May
receive

THE SEVENTH RAY: REV]

THE SEVENTH RAY: REVEALER OF THE NEW AGE

*From the Writings of
Alice A. Bailey
and
The Tibetan Master, Djwhal Khul*

LUCIS PUBLISHING COMPANY
New York

LUCIS PRESS, LTD.
London

This compilation is extracted from books by Alice A. Bailey for which the Lucis Trust holds copyrights.

First Printing, 1995

ISBN No. 0-85330-141-7

The Lucis Publishing Company is a non-profit organization owned by the Lucis Trust. No royalties are paid on this book.

LUCIS PUBLISHING COMPANY
120 Wall Street
New York, N.Y. 10005

LUCIS PRESS LTD.
Suite 54
3 Whitehall Court
London SW1A 2EF
ENGLAND

MANUFACTURED IN THE UNITED STATES OF AMERICA
BY FORT ORANGE PRESS, INC., ALBANY, N.Y.

THE GREAT INVOCATION

**From the point of Light within the Mind of God
Let light stream forth into the minds of men.
Let Light descend on Earth.**

**From the point of Love within the Heart of God
Let love stream forth into the hearts of men.
May Christ return to Earth.**

**From the centre where the Will of God is known
Let purpose guide the little wills of men—
The purpose which the Masters know and serve.**

**From the centre which we call the race of men
Let the Plan of Love and Light work out
And may it seal the door where evil dwells.**

**Let Light and Love and Power restore the
Plan on Earth.**

"The above Invocation or Prayer does not belong to any person or group but to all Humanity. The beauty and the strength of this Invocation lies in its simplicity, and in its expression of certain central truths which all men, innately and normally, accept—the truth of the existence of a basic Intelligence to Whom we vaguely give the name of God; the truth that behind all outer seeming, the motivating power of the universe is Love; the truth that a great Individuality came to earth, called by Christians, the Christ, and embodied that love so that we could understand; the truth that both love and intelligence are effects of what is called the Will of God; and finally the self-evident truth that only through humanity itself can the Divine Plan work out."

Alice A. Bailey

EXTRACT FROM A STATEMENT BY THE TIBETAN

Published August 1934

Suffice it to say, that I am a Tibetan disciple of a certain degree, and this tells you but little, for all are disciples from the humblest aspirant up to, and beyond, the Christ Himself. I live in a physical body like other men, on the borders of Tibet, and at times (from the exoteric standpoint) preside over a large group of Tibetan lamas, when my other duties permit. It is this fact that has caused it to be reported that I am an abbot of this particular lamasery. Those associated with me in the work of the Hierarchy (and all true disciples are associated in this work) know me by still another name and office. A.A.B. knows who I am and recognises me by two of my names.

I am a brother of yours, who has travelled a little longer upon the Path than has the average student, and has therefore incurred greater responsibilities. I am one who has wrestled and fought his way into a greater measure of light than has the aspirant who will read this article, and I must therefore act as a transmitter of the light, no matter what the cost. I am not an old man, as age counts among the teachers, yet I am not young or inexperienced. My work is to teach and spread the knowledge of the Ageless Wisdom wherever I can find a response, and I have been doing this for many years. I seek also to help the Master M. and the Master K.H. whenever opportunity offers, for I have been long connected with Them and with Their work. In all the above, I have told you much; yet at the same time I have told you nothing which would lead you to offer me that blind obedience and the foolish devotion which the emotional aspirant offers to the Guru and Master Whom he is as yet unable to contact. Nor will he make that desired contact until he has transmuted emotional devotion into unselfish service to humanity—not to the Master.

The books that I have written are sent out with no claim for their acceptance. They may, or may not, be correct, true and useful. It is for you to ascertain their truth by right practice and by the exercise of the intuition. Neither I nor A.A.B. is the least interested in having them acclaimed as inspired writings, or in having anyone speak of them (with bated breath) as being the work of one of the Masters. If they present truth in such a way that it follows sequentially upon that already offered in the world teachings, if the information given raises the aspiration and the will-to-serve from the plane of the emotions to that of the mind (the plane whereon the masters can be found) then they will have served their purpose. If the teaching conveyed calls forth a response from the illumined mind of the worker in the world, and brings a flashing forth of his intuition, then let that teaching be accepted. But not otherwise. If the statements meet with eventual corroboration, or are deemed true under the test of the Law of Correspondences, then that is well and good. But should this not be so, let not the student accept what is said.

TABLE OF CONTENTS

	PAGE
FOREWORD	XI
Chapter 1: GENERAL INTRODUCTORY STATEMENTS	1
a. The Seven Rays	
b. The Seventh Ray	
Chapter 2: TRANSITION FROM A SIXTH TO A SEVENTH RAY CYCLE	16
Chapter 3: THE THREE DEPARTMENTS OF HIERARCHY	63
a. The Solar and Planetary Hierarchies	
b. The Work of the Mahachohan	
c. The Seventh Ray Ashram	
Chapter 4: ASTROLOGY AND THE SEVENTH RAY	82
Chapter 5: THE PSYCHOLOGY OF NATIONS	101
a. Seventh Ray Nations	
b. Seventh Ray Influences Via Planetary Rulers	
Chapter 6: THE SEVENTH RAY MANIFESTING THROUGH THE INDIVIDUAL	105
a. General Traits and Tendencies	
b. Instructions to Individual Members of the Tibetan's Seed Group	
Chapter 7: ESOTERIC HEALING AND THE SEVENTH RAY	128
Chapter 8: MEDITATION—THE SEVENTH RAY IMPACT	136
Chapter 9: THE SEVENTH RAY AND INITIATION	146
Chapter 10: EFFECTS OF THE INCOMING SEVENTH RAY	157
a. Masonry	
b. The Mineral Kingdom	
c. Animals	
d. Devas	
e. Spiritualism	
f. Future Unfoldment: The Fusion of Spirit and Matter	

REFERENCE INDEX

BOOKS BY THE TIBETAN (DJWHAL KHUL) and ALICE A. BAILEY

Book Abr.	Title	First Edition	Reference Edition		Pages
IHS	*Initiation, Human and Solar*	1922	16th	1992	240
LOM	*Letters on Occult Meditation*	1922	15th	1993	375
CF	*A Treatise on Cosmic Fire*	1925	13th	1989	1367
WM	*A Treatise on White Magic*	1934	17th	1991	705
DINAI	*Discipleship in the New Age, Vol. I*	1944	12th	1989	847
DINAII	*Discipleship in the New Age, Vol. II*	1955	8th	1994	818
DN	*The Destiny of the Nations*	1949	8th	1990	161
GLA	*Glamour: A World Problem*	1950	9th	1995	290
TEL	*Telepathy and the Etheric Vehicle*	1950	11th	1995	219
EXH	*The Externalisation of the Hierarchy*	1957	8th	1989	744
	A Treatise on the Seven Rays:				
EPI	*Esoteric Psychology, Vol. I*	1936	12th	1991	460
EPII	*Esoteric Psychology, Vol. II*	1942	10th	1988	818
EA	*Esoteric Astrology*	1951	14th	1989	742
EH	*Esoteric Healing*	1953	13th	1993	770
RI	*The Rays and the Initiations*	1960	9th	1993	820

It might first be stated that the main problem of today is brought about by the fact that two rays of great potency are functioning simultaneously. As yet their effects are so equally balanced that a situation is brought about which is described in the ancient archives in the following terms: "A time of rending, when the mountains, which have sheltered, fall from their high places, and the voices of men are lost in the crash and thunder of the fall." Such periods come only at rare and long intervals, and each time they come a peculiarly significant period of divine activity is ushered in; old things pass entirely away, yet the ancient landmarks are restored. The seventh Ray of Ceremonial Order or Ritual is coming into manifestation. The sixth Ray of Idealism or of Abstract Visioning is slowly passing out. The seventh ray will bring into expression that which was visioned and that which constituted the ideals of the preceding cycle of sixth ray activity. One ray prepares the way for another ray, and the reason for the manifestation of one ray or another is dependent upon the Plan and divine Purpose. It is not often that two rays follow each other in a regular numerical sequence, such as is now happening. When this does happen, there eventuates a rapid following of effect upon cause, and this today can provide the basis for an assured hope.

Esoteric Psychology, Vol. I, pp. 357-58

One of the inevitable effects of seventh ray energy will be to relate and weld into a closer synthesis the four kingdoms in nature. This must be done as preparatory to the long fore-ordained work of humanity which is to be the distributing agency for spiritual energy to the three subhuman kingdoms. This is the major task of service which the fourth kingdom, through its incarnating souls, has undertaken. The radiation from the fourth kingdom will some day be so potent and far-reaching that its effects will permeate down into the very depths of the created phenomenal world, even into the mineral kingdom. Then we shall see the results to which the great initiate, Paul, refers when he speaks of the whole creation waiting for the manifestation of the Sons of God. That manifestation is that of radiating glory and power and love.

The Destiny of the Nations, p. 124

FOREWORD

The collaboration of the Tibetan Master Djwhal Khul and Alice A. Bailey over a period of thirty years, from 1919 to 1949, resulted in the publication of a body of teaching on the Ageless Wisdom which the Tibetan foresaw would be most relevant to the group of disciples working at the close of the twentieth century.

Humanity is living through the period of transition between the outgoing Piscean age, governed by the sixth Ray of Devotion and Idealism, and the incoming Aquarian age, ruled by the seventh Ray of Order and Organisation. As an aid to men and women endeavouring to prepare themselves for discipleship service during this time, the Tibetan suggested the preparation of a compilation of all his statements on the seventh ray found throughout the books he wrote with Alice Bailey.

The seventh Ray of Ceremonial Order is one of seven rays of energy which demonstrate the seven qualities of Deity, and which consequently have a sevenfold effect upon the matter and forms found throughout the universe. In the age which is rapidly coming into being, the seventh ray will be the dominant energy for some 2000 years. Thus it becomes imperative that students of the Ageless Wisdom gain a deeper understanding of the seventh ray, its nature and potency. In fact, as forecast in Letters on Occult Meditation by Alice A. Bailey, the teaching on the seventh ray will form a part of the curriculum of the future occult schools.

As humanity gains greater responsiveness to the energy of order and organisation of the seventh ray—the ray of "ritualistic decency" — an ordered beauty and rhythm will begin to demonstrate in all aspects of physical plane living. In the hope that this compilation may contribute to a recognition of new opportunities for group service, we are pleased to offer The Seventh Ray: Revealer of the New Age.

Lucis Publishing Company, April 1995

CHAPTER ONE
GENERAL INTRODUCTORY STATEMENTS
The Seven Rays

WE are told that seven great rays exist in the cosmos. In our solar system only one of these seven great rays is in operation. The seven sub-divisions constitute the "seven rays" which, wielded by our solar Logos, form the basis of endless variations in His system of worlds. These seven rays may be described as the seven channels through which all being in His solar system flows, the seven predominant characteristics or modifications of life, for it is not to humanity only that these rays apply, but to the seven kingdoms as well. In fact there is nothing in the whole solar system, at whatever stage of evolution it may stand, which does not belong and has not always belonged to one or other of the seven rays....

EPI 163

The seven rays are the sum total of the divine Consciousness, of the universal Mind; They might be regarded as seven intelligent Entities through Whom the plan is working out. They embody divine purpose, express the qualities required for the materialising of that purpose, and They create the forms and are the forms through which the divine idea can be carried forward to completion. Symbolically, They may be regarded as constituting the brain of the divine Heavenly Man. They correspond to the ventricles of the brain, to the seven centres within the brain, to the seven centres of force, and to the seven major glands which determine the quality of the physical body. They are the conscious executors of divine purpose; They are the seven Breaths, animating all forms which have been created by Them to carry out the plan.

It may perhaps be easier to understand the relation of

the seven rays to Deity if we remember that man himself (being made in the image of God) is a seven-fold being, capable of seven states of consciousness, expressive of the seven principles or basic qualities which enable him to be aware of the seven planes upon which he is, consciously or unconsciously, functioning. He is a septenate at all times, but his objective is to be consciously aware of all the states of being, to express consciously all the qualities, and to function freely on all the planes.

The seven ray Beings, unlike man, are fully conscious and entirely aware of the purpose and the Plan. They are "ever in deep meditation", and have reached the point where, through Their advanced stage of development, They are "impelled toward fulfillment". They are fully self-conscious and group-conscious; They are the sum total of the universal mind; They are "awake and active". Their goal and Their purpose is such that it is idle for us to speculate about it, for the highest point of achievement for man is the lowest point for Them. These seven Rays, Breaths and Heavenly Men have the task of wrestling with matter in order to subjugate it to divine purpose, and the goal—as far as one can sense it—is to subject the material forms to the play of the life aspect, thus producing those qualities which will carry the will of God to completion. They are therefore the sum total of all the souls within the solar system, and Their activity produces all forms; according to the nature of the form so will be the grade of consciousness. Through the seven rays, the life or spirit aspect flows, cycling through every kingdom in nature and producing thus all states of consciousness in all fields of awareness.

For the purpose of this treatise students will have to accept the hypothesis that every human being is swept into manifestation on the impulse of some ray, and is coloured by that particular ray quality, which determines the form aspect, indicates the way he should go, and enables him (by the time the third initiation is reached) to have sensed and then to have cooperated with his ray purpose. After the third initiation he begins to sense the synthetic purpose towards which all the seven rays are working; but as this treatise is written for aspirants and disciples, and not for initiates of the third degree, it is needless to speculate upon this ultimate destiny.

The human soul is a synthesis of material energy, qualified by intelligent consciousness, plus the spiritual energy which is, in its turn, qualified by one of the seven ray types.

Thus the human being emerges, a son of God, incarnate in form, with one hand (as the Old Commentary says) holding firmly to the rock of matter and with the other hand plunged into a sea of love. An ancient scripture puts it thus:

> "When the right hand of the man of matter grasps the flower of life and plucks it for himself, the left hand remains in emptiness.
>
> "When the right hand of the man of matter grasps the golden lotus of the soul, the left descends seeking the flower of life, though he seeks it not for selfish ends.
>
> "When the right hands holds the golden lotus firm and the left hand grasps the flower of life, man finds himself to be the seven-leaved plant which flowers on earth and flowers before the Throne of God."

The purpose of Deity, as it is known to the Creator, is totally unknown to all save the higher initiates. But the purpose of each ray Life may be sensed and defined, subject of course to the limitations of the human mind and to the inadequacy of words. The planned activity of every ray qualifies every form found within its body of manifestation.

We come now to a technical statement which must be accepted for the sake of argument, being incapable of proof. All the Lords of the rays create a body of expression, and thus the seven planets have come into being. These are their major expressions.

> The Sun (Veiling Vulcan)
> Jupiter
> Saturn
> Mercury
> Venus
> Mars
> The Moon

The energies of these seven Lives however are not confined to their planetary expressions, but sweep around the confines of the solar system just as the life impulses of a human being—his vital forces, his desire impulses, and his mental energies—sweep throughout his body, bringing the various organs into activity and enabling him to carry out his intent, to live his life, and to fulfill the objective for which he created his body of manifestation.

Each of the seven kingdoms in nature reacts to the energy of some particular ray Life. Each of the seven planes similarly reacts; each septenate in nature vibrates to one or another of the initial septenates, for the seven rays establish that process which assigns the limits of influence of all forms. They are that which determines all things, and when I use these words I indicate the necessity of Law. Law is the will of the seven Deities, making its impression upon substance in order to produce a specific intent through the method of the evolutionary process.

EPI 59-62

It is of major interest for us to know something about the energies and forces which are producing the present international situation and presenting the complex problems with which the United Nations are confronted. In the last analysis, all history is the record of the effects of these energies or radiations (rays, in other words) as they play upon humanity in its many varying stages of evolutionary development. These stages extend all the way from those of primeval humanity to our modern civilisation; all that has happened is the result of these energies, pouring cyclically through nature and through that part of nature which we call the human kingdom.

To understand what is today taking place we must recognise that these energies are seven in number. They are called by many names in many different lands, but for our purposes the following seven names will be used:

1. The energy of Will, Purpose or Power, called in Christian lands the energy of the Will of God.

2. The energy of Love-Wisdom, called frequently the Love of God.

3. The energy of Active Intelligence, called the Mind of God.

4. The energy of Harmony through Conflict, affecting greatly the human family.

5. The energy of Concrete Knowledge or Science, so potent at this time.

6. The energy of Devotion or Idealism, producing the current ideologies.

7. The energy of Ceremonial Order, producing the new forms of civilisation.

These energies are ceaselessly playing on humanity, producing changes, expressing themselves through successive civilisations and cultures, and fashioning the many races and nations....

This teaching anent the seven rays remains a profitless speculation unless it is susceptible of investigation, of eventual proof and of general as well as particular usefulness. Too much is written at this time which will have to be relegated to the discard as useless, as not warranting acceptance as a possible hypothesis and as not demonstrating a truth which can be proved....

DN 3-4

Two rays are largely the goal of human endeavour, the first ray and the second ray. One ray is the goal of the deva or angel evolution, the third ray. All these three rays contact the two poles, and the attainment of the goal at the end of the cycle marks the achievement of the solar Logos. This again is hidden in mystery. The seventh ray and the first ray are very closely allied, with the third ray linking them, so that we have the relation expressed thus—1. 3. 7. There is a close association also between rays 2. 4. 6., with the fifth ray in a peculiar position, as a central point of attainment, the home of the ego or soul, the embodied plane of mind, the point of consummation for the personality, and the reflection in the three worlds of the threefold monad.

Ray I.... Will, demonstrating as power in the unfolding of the Plan of the Logos.

Ray III.. Adaptability of activity with intelligence. This ray was the dominant one in the past solar system; it is the foundation or basis of this system, and is controlled by the Mahachohan.

Ray VII..Ceremonial ritual or organisation. This is the reflection on the physical plane of the two above and is likewise connected with the Mahachohan. It controls the elemental forces and the involutionary process and the form side of the three kingdoms in nature. It holds hid the secret of physical colour and sound. It is the law....

These two groups of rays might be related to each other as follows:

Rays l. 3. 7 are the great rays connected with the form, with the evolutionary process, with the intelligent functioning of the system, and with the laws controlling the life in all forms in all the kingdoms in nature.

Rays 2. 4. 6 are the rays connected with the inner life, expanding through those forms—the rays of motive, aspiration and sacrifice. Rays pre-eminently of quality.

Rays. 1. 3. 7 deal with things concrete and with the functioning of matter and form from the lowest plane to the highest.

Rays 2. 4. 6 deal with things abstract, with spiritual expression through the medium of form.

Ray 5.....forms the connecting link of the intelligence.

EPI 88-89

The Seventh Ray

RAY VII.—This is the energy of Ceremonial Order. It is an expression of the will which drives through into outer manifestation; it is that which embodies both the periphery and the point at the centre. It is the will to "ritualistic synthesis", if I might so word it. It is Necessity which is the prime conditioning factor of the divine nature—the necessity to express itself; the necessity to manifest in an orderly rhythmic manner; the necessity to embrace "that which is above and that which is below" and, through the medium of this activity, to produce beauty, order, perfect wholes and right relationships. It is the driving energy which Being emanates as It appears and takes form and lives. It is the *Will towards Expression.* Today, as regards humanity, its highest expression is organisation.

EA 601

The Lord of Ceremonial Order or Magic is now coming into power and is slowly but surely making His pressure felt. His influence is most potent upon the physical plane, for there is a close numerical interrelation between (for instance) the Lord of the seventh ray and the seventh plane, the physical, just as the seventh root race will see complete conformity to and a perfect expression of law and order. This ray of order and its incoming is partially responsible for the present tendency in world affairs toward governmental dictatorship and the imposed control of a central governing body.

EPI 25-26

"When the light of the seven Rays is blended with that of the seventh Ray, then light supernal can be known."

The implications attendant upon this...point are amazing at the first glance, and they demand an immediate recognition of the two factors of time and space. The significances which are implicit in this point may be clearer if I paraphrase the statement and thus give you a sense of significance which will give you understanding. When the energy of the light of all the rays can express themselves through the medium of the seventh ray, then the highest aspect of the divine light can penetrate down into the physical plane. This must be obviously a most difficult statement for you to grasp, but it is also a statement of fundamental truth.

In an earlier instruction I pointed out that three ideas were involved in grasping the significance of these points of revelation and—once you have grasped them—they are beautifully clear and simple. The *Procedure* required for the manifestation of "light supernal" takes place when a transitory point of synthesis is reached and the seven energies are blended into one great energetic Light. These seven energies have ever, unitedly, created the "light supernal" upon the highest levels of divine expression, but that revealing light only finds *Location* when the seventh Ray of Ceremonial Order is active and in process of manifestation in the three worlds, and necessarily, therefore, upon the seventh plane, the physical plane. Such a manifestation inevitably takes place in moments of planetary crisis, when the seventh ray is active and when the Sun is in Aquarius. Such a combination of relationships is being established now, for the seventh ray is rapidly coming into manifestation and the Sun is in Aquarius, for the Aquarian Age is just beginning. The *Objective* of this combination (which has occurred six times during this period of the fifth root race) is to bring about illumination and the establishment of order upon the Earth. The first indication of the possibility of the effectiveness of these divine proposals was the giving out of the New Invocation; its potency was so great that right conditions *had* to be considered before its enunciation was possible. That was the first step in the planned precipitation of the "light supernal"; the second step will be the reappearance of the Great Lord, Who will act as the lens through which the light can be focussed and adapted to human need. Conditions are rapidly being brought about whereby this great event of light distribution will be possible. The Christ can and does function now upon the atmic plane and embodies within Himself the great Point of Revelation which has been expressed by me in the words: "The Will is an expression of the Law of Sacrifice." The invocation now mounting from humanity to that high Place where dwells the Christ is, at this time, focussed in or originates upon the plane of the emotions; because of this, we find the words in the Scriptures that at the end of the age "the *Desire* of all Nations" will come forth. The movement to bring Him—from the angle of the masses— emanates, therefore, from the astral plane. The plans for His coming are being laid in the higher correspondence of that plane, the buddhic plane or the plane of pure reason.

The motivating power for His coming is being provided by all disciples and initiates; it is therefore a joint movement, qualified by the desire and the motivation of the united Hierarchy and Humanity; this Invocation cannot consequently be denied. Astrologically, the time is propitious; from the planetary angle, great and momentous events are imminent, as the planetary Logos is taking a cosmic initiation; the energy which produces order and which magically brings spirit and matter together (the energy of the seventh ray) is already organising human affairs and these three great coinciding events in time and space make it possible for the seventh ray energies to reach a high point of fused activity and of blended cooperation.

The result will be the creation of a direct channel for the precipitation of "light supernal" into the three worlds and its dominant focussing upon the physical plane. Thus will be brought about the new civilisation and the new world order, and the new approach to divinity will be rendered possible; the initial steps will then be taken to create the "new heavens and the new earth". You will need here to discriminate carefully between symbols and facts; more, I need not here indicate.

DINAII 425-27

We shall now express the ray purpose in the form of an ancient teaching preserved on leaves that are so old that the writing is slowly fading. I now translate it into modern language though much is lost thereby....

The Seventh Purpose of Deity

Ray VII. Ceremonial Order or Magic

"Let the Temple of the Lord be built", the seventh great Angel cried. Then to their places in the north, the south, the west and east, seven great sons of God moved with measured pace and took their seats. The work of building thus began.

The doors were closed. The light shone dim. The temple walls could not be seen. The seven were silent and their forms were veiled. The time had not arrived for the breaking forth of light. The Word could not be uttered. Only between the seven Forms the work went on. A silent call went forth from each to each. Yet still the temple door stayed shut.

As time went on, the sounds of life were heard. The

door was opened, and the door was shut. Each time it opened, the power within the temple grew; each time the light waxed stronger, for one by one the sons of men entered the temple, passed from north to south, from west to east and in the centre of the heart found light, found understanding and the power to work. They entered through the door; they passed before the Seven; they raised the temple's veil and entered into life.

The temple grew in beauty. Its lines, its walls, its decorations, and its height and depth and breadth slowly emerged and entered into light.

Out from the east, the Word went forth: Open the door to all the sons of men who come from all the darkened valleys of the land and seek the temple of the Lord. Give them the light. Unveil the inner shrine, and through the work of all the craftsmen of the Lord extend the temple's walls and thus irradiate the world. Sound forth the Word creative and raise the dead to life.

Thus shall the temple of the light be carried from heaven to earth. Thus shall its walls be reared upon the great plains of the world of men. Thus shall the light reveal and nurture all the dreams of men.

Then shall the Master in the east awaken those who are asleep. Then shall the warden in the west test and try all the true seekers after light. Then shall the warden in the south instruct and aid the blind. Then shall the gate into the north remain wide open, for there the unseen Master stands with welcoming hand and understanding heart, to lead the pilgrims to the east where the true light shines forth.

"Why this opening of the temple?" demand the greater Seven. "Because the work is ready; the craftsmen are prepared. God has created in the light. His sons can now create. What can else be done?"

"Naught!" came the answer from the greater Seven. "Let the work proceed. Let the sons of God create."

These words will be noted by many as of deep significance and as indicating a wide intention (during the coming cycle) to open the door wide into the temple of the hidden mystery to man. One by one we shall undergo the esoteric and spiritual counterpart of the psychological factor which is called "a mental test". That test will demonstrate a man's usefulness in mental work and power, it will show his capacity to build thoughtforms and to vitalise them. This I dealt with in A Treatise on White Magic, and the relation of that treatise to the magical work of the seventh ray and its cycle of activity will become increasingly apparent. A Treatise on White Magic is an attempt to lay down the rules for training and for work which will make it possible for the candidate to the mysteries to enter the temple and to take his place as a creative worker and thus aid in the magical work of the Lord of the Temple.

The names whereby this ray Lord is known are many, and their meaning is of prime significance today. The work of the future can be seen from a study of these names.

> The Unveiled Magician
> The Worker in the Magical Art
> The Creator of the Form
> The Bestower of Light from the Second Lord
> The Manipulator of the Wand
> The Watcher in the East
> The Custodian of the Seventh Plane
> The Invoker of Wrath
> The Keeper of the Magical Word
> The Temple Guardian
> The Representative of God
> The One Who lifts to Life

General Introductory Statements

The Lord of Death
The One Who feeds the Sacred Fire
The Whirling Sphere
The Sword of the Initiator
The Divine Alchemical Worker
The Builder of the Square
The Orienting Force
The Fiery Unifier
The Key to the Mystery
The Expression of the Will
The Revealer of Beauty

This ray Lord has a peculiar power on earth and on the physical plane of divine manifestation. His usefulness to His six Brothers is therefore apparent. He makes Their work appear. He is the most active of all the rays in this world period, and is never out of manifestation for more than fifteen hundred years. It is almost as if He whirled in and out of active work under a very rapid cycle, and His closest relation, symbolically, is to His Brethren of the second and fifth rays in this world period.

He builds (using second ray cooperation) through the power of thought (thus cooperating with the Lord of the fifth ray and on the physical plane, which is His own essential and peculiar sphere). In another world period His relation with the other ray Lords may undergo change, but at this time His work will be more easily understood when He is recognised as aiding the building Lord of the second ray and utilising the energies of the Lord of concrete thought.

The aphorisms embodying His qualities run as follows, and were esoterically whispered into His ears when He "left the most high place and descended into the seventh sphere to carry out the work assigned".

1. Take thy tools with thee, brother of the building light. Carve deep. Construct and shape the living stone.
    Quality....power to create.

2. Choose well thy workers. Love them all. Pick six to do thy will. Remain the seventh in the east. Yet call the world to enter into that which thou shalt build. Blend all together in the will of God.
    Quality....power to cooperate

3. Sit in the centre and the east as well. Move not from there. Send out thy force to do thy will and gather back thy forces. Use well the power of thought. Sit still.
    Quality.....power to think.

4. See all parts enter into the purpose. Build towards beauty, brother Lord. Make all colours bright and clear. See to the inner glory. Build the shrine well. Use care.
    Quality....revelation of the beauty of God.

5. Watch well thy thought. Enter at will into the mind of God. Pluck thence the power, the plan, the part to play. Reveal the mind of God.
    Quality.....mental power.

6. Stay in the east. The five have given thee a friendly Word. I, the sixth, tell thee to use it on the dead. Revive the dead. Build forms anew. Guard well that Word. Make all men seek it for themselves.
    Quality....power to vivify.

EPI 62, 83-87

It was the realisation of the present world need for illumined thinkers and subjective workers which prompted Those Who guide so to direct the incoming spiritual energies that the formation of the esoteric groups everywhere came about; it led also to the publication of the mass of mystical and Oriental literature on meditation and allied topics which has flooded the world today. Hence also the effort that I, a worker on the inner side of life, am making to reach the newer psychology in this treatise, and so show to man what is his equipment and how well suited he is to the work for which he has been created, and which he has

General Introductory Statements

as yet failed to comprehend. The force and the effect of the seventh ray influence will, however, reveal to him the magical work, and the next twenty-five hundred years will bring about so much change and make possible the working of so many so-called "miracles" that even the outer appearance of the world will be profoundly altered; the vegetation and the animal life will be modified and developed, and much that is latent in the forms of both kingdoms will be brought into expression through the freer flow and the more intelligent manipulation of the energies which create and constitute all forms. The world has been changed beyond belief during the past five hundred years, and during the next two hundred years the changes will be still more rapid and deep-seated, for the growth of the intellectual powers of man is gathering momentum, and Man, the Creator, is coming into possession of His powers.

EP1 82-83

CHAPTER TWO

TRANSITION FROM A SIXTH TO A SEVENTH RAY CYCLE

Certain great readjustments are going on in that centre [humanity, *Editors*], for it is beginning to conform at long last to divine intention. I have elsewhere pointed out that for the first time in the long history of human development, energy from Shamballa has made a direct impact upon this third planetary centre. This is not due entirely to the point in evolution attained by mankind; this attainment is only a secondary reason or cause. It is due to the will of Sanat Kumara Himself as He prepares for a certain cosmic initiation. This initiation requires the reorganisation of the energies flowing through and composing that "centre which we call the race of men"; this creates a rearrangement within the centre itself, and thus brings into manifested expression certain aspects and qualities—always inherent in those energies—which have not hitherto been recognised. This creative crisis has been made possible by three major happenings:

1. The conclusion of a twenty-five thousand year cycle or movement around what is called the lesser zodiac. This connotes a major cycle of experience in the life of our planetary Logos. It is related to the interplay between the planetary Logos and the solar Logos as the latter responds to energies emanating from the twelve zodiacal constellations.

2. The end of the Piscean Age. This simply means that the energies coming from Pisces during the last two thousand years are now being rapidly superseded by energies coming from Aquarius. These result in major changes in the life of the planetary Logos and potently affect His body of manifestation through

Transformation from a Sixth to a Seventh Ray Cycle

the medium of His three major centres: Shamballa, the Hierarchy and Humanity.

3. The increasingly dominant activity of the seventh Ray of Order or Ceremonial Magic, as it is somewhat erroneously called. This ray is now coming into manifestation and is in close cooperation with the two above factors; it produces also the lessening of the power of the sixth Ray of Idealism. This has had a long cycle and has greatly hastened the evolutionary process; it demonstrates its effective work in the emergence today of the great world ideologies. I am necessarily considering these energies only in relation to the human consciousness.

RI 550-51

It is apparent therefore that the day of opportunity is with us, and that the coming generation can, if it so wishes, perform the magical work with many of the factors present which will tend to produce satisfactory results. The fifth ray is passing out, but its influence can still be felt; the third ray is at full meridian, and the seventh ray is rapidly coming into right activity. Much will consequently occur to make man successful, provided he can preserve constantly a right orientation, purity of motive and of life, a stabilised and receptive emotional body and that inner alignment which will make his personality a true vehicle for his soul or self.

WM 511-12

We have now to deal with the influence of a force that is waning and passing out of dominance, that of the sixth Ray of Devotion or Idealism. It will not be possible to predicate much anent it, beyond pointing out certain general ideas which may be of value in the contemplation of ray cycles in general.

These ray influences work through their focal points in all cases (macrocosmic and microcosmic) and these are the etheric centres. The centres, in the case of all Beings, are ever seven in number, and are composed of deva and human units in group activity, or of force vortices which contain in latency, and hold in ordered activity, cells with the potentiality of human manifestation. Forget not the occult truism that all forms of existence pass at one stage of their career through the human kingdom.

Cosmic, or extra-systemic rays, impinge upon or circulate via centres found on the second cosmic ether, but which, at the present stage of objectivity, become systemically visible in the fourth cosmic ether, the buddhic.

One permanent cosmic Ray is the ray of our Logos Himself, and the subrays of this ray permeate His entire system. Six other cosmic Rays, animating other systems, influence ours, finding their reflections in the subrays of our logoic ray. To these six cosmic influences our Heavenly Men respond. They absorb the influence, being centres in the body logoic, pass it through Their schemes, circulate it through Their Own centres (chains), and transmit it on to other schemes, coloring it with Their Own peculiar shade and qualifying it by Their Own peculiar tone or note. The whole system of ray influence, or radiatory warmth, considered both physically and psychically, is one of an intricate circulation and interaction. The radiation or vibration passes in ordered cycles from its originating source, the One Ray, or systemic Logos, to the different centres in His body. Viewed from the physical standpoint this ray force is the energising factor in matter. Viewed from the psychical point of view it is the qualitative faculty. From scheme to scheme, from chain to chain, and from globe to globe, this force or quality passes and circulates, both adding, and at the same time abstracting, and returns to its focal point with two noticeable differences:

Transformation from a Sixth to a Seventh Ray Cycle 19

a. The radiatory heat is intensified.
b. The qualitative character or colour is increased....

As the ray influence passes away from a race or a planet, a scheme or a solar system, it must not be supposed that it is completely abrogated; it has simply passed beyond the periphery of whatever ring-pass-not it was energising, and the force of its influence is being focussed elsewhere. The original recipient becomes a channel, or transmitting agent, and not so much an absorber or container. Words again are handicapping us, and proving their inadequacy to express an idea. What the student should recognise is that during a cycle of ray influence, the object of its immediate attention receives and absorbs it, and transmutes it according to its need, and not so much therefore is available for transmission. When the cycle is drawing to a close more and more of the ray influence or magnetism will be felt elsewhere, until practically all of it will be passed on unabsorbed.

This is what is beginning to happen in relation to this sixth Ray of Devotion. Egos who are on that particular ray will take form elsewhere on other globes, and in other chains, and not so much on our planet. The vibrations of that ray will quiet down as far as we are concerned, and find increased activity elsewhere. To phrase it otherwise, our planet and all thereon will become positive and non-receptive, and will temporarily repulse this particular type of force. A psychical manifestation of this can be seen in the dying down of what is called *Christian* enthusiasm. This ray, on which the Chohan Jesus may be found, will no longer pour its force to the same extent into the form He built, and it will necessarily slowly but surely disintegrate, having served its purpose for close on two thousand years. Later again the same force will be felt returning, and a new form will be found slowly coming into being, but along more adequate lines.

It will consequently be apparent how the knowledge of these cycles, and of the force manifestation or obscuration of a ray will eventually lead to a working with the Law, and to an intelligent co-operation with the plan of evolution. It might here be stated that the seven Kumaras (the four exoteric and the three esoteric) cooperate with this Law, and work exoterically, or esoterically according to the ray in power, with the exception of the first Kumara, the Logos of our scheme, Who—being the synthesising point for all—remains ever in objective activity.

It is this ray activity which governs the obscuration or manifestation of a system, and a scheme with all that is included in these manifestations. Hence the emphasis laid in all occult books on the study of cycles, and on the differentiation of the one hundred years of Brahma into its component parts. In this knowledge lies hid the mystery of Being itself, of electrical force, and of fohatic synthesis.

I will make no more comments on the future effects of the ray which is passing into temporary obscuration as far as we are concerned. We shall later take up at greater length than has been possible with the other rays, the subject of the seventh type of force now coming into power, and which is therefore a vital factor in the immediate evolution of man.

CF 436-40

We come now to a consideration of the forces which are prevailing at the present time and hence have a supreme interest in connection with what I now have to say. It might first be stated that the main problem of today is brought about by the fact that two rays of great potency are functioning simultaneously. As yet their effects are so equally balanced that a situation is brought about which is described in the ancient archives in the following terms: "A time of rending, when the mountains, which have sheltered, fall from their high places, and the voices of men are lost in the crash and thunder of the fall." Such periods come only at rare and long intervals, and each time they come a peculiarly significant period of divine activity is ushered in; old things pass entirely away, yet the ancient landmarks are restored. The seventh Ray of Ceremonial Order or Ritual is coming into manifestation. The sixth Ray of Idealism or of Abstract Visioning is slowly passing out. The seventh ray will bring into expression that which was visioned and that which constituted the ideals of the preceding cycle of sixth ray activity. One ray prepares the way for another ray, and the reason for the manifestation of one ray or another is dependent upon the Plan and divine Purpose. It is not often that two rays follow each other in a regular numerical sequence, such as is now happening. When this does happen, there eventuates a rapid following of effect upon cause, and this today can provide the basis for an assured hope.

The sixth ray influence served to attract men's minds towards an ideal, such as that of individual sacrifice or service, and the mystical vision was the high water mark of the period; the numerous guiding mystics of the Occident and the Orient have appeared. The seventh ray influence will in time produce the magician, but in this age the magician will be predominantly in the class of white magic (not as in Atlantean days, when the predominance was on the side of selfish or black magic). The white magician works with the forces of nature and swings them back into control of advanced humanity. This can already be seen working out through the activity of the scientists which the latter end of the last century and this twentieth century have produced. That much of their magical work has been turned into selfish channels by the tendency of this materialistic age, and that many of their wise and true discoveries in the realm of energy are today adapted to ends which serve men's hatred or love of self, is equally true. But this in no way militates against the wonder of their achievements. When the motive is transmuted from pure scientific interest to love of the divine revelation, and when service to the race is the determining force, then we shall see the true white magic. Hence therefore the need to turn the mystic into the occultist, and to train the modern aspirant in right motive, mind control and brotherly love—all of which must and will express themselves through harmlessness. The most potent force in the world today is harmlessness. I speak not of non-resistance, but of that positive attitude of mind which thinks no evil. He who thinks no evil and harms naught is a citizen of God's world.

The following relations between the sixth and seventh rays should be held clearly in mind, and students should grasp the relation of the immediate past to the immediate future, and see in this relation the working out of God's Plan and the coming salvation of the race:

a. The sixth ray fostered the vision.
   The seventh ray will materialise that which was visioned.

b. The sixth ray produced the mystic as its culminating type of aspirant.
   The seventh ray will develop the magician who works in the field of white magic.

c. The sixth ray, as part of the evolutionary plan, led to separations, to nationalism, and to sectarianism, due to the selective nature of the mind and its tendency to divide and separate.
   The seventh ray will lead to fusion and synthesis, for its energy is of the type which blends spirit and matter.

d. The sixth ray activity led to the formation of bands of disciples, working in groups but not in close relation, and subject to internal dissension, based on personality reactions.

The seventh ray will train and send forth groups of initiates, working in close unison with the Plan and with each other.

e. The sixth ray brought the sense of duality to a humanity which regarded itself as a physical unity. Of this attitude the academic materialistic psychologists are the exponents.

The seventh ray will inaugurate the sense of a higher unity; first, that of the integrated personality for the masses, and secondly, that of the fusion of soul and body for the world aspirants.

f. The sixth ray differentiates that aspect of the universal electrical energy which we know as modern electricity, produced to serve man's material needs.

The seventh ray period will familiarise man with that type of electrical phenomena which produce the coordination of all forms.

g. The sixth ray influence produced the emergence in men's minds of the following knowledges:
  1. Knowledge of physical plane light and electricity.
  2. Among the esotericists and spiritualists of the world, knowledge of the existence of the astral light.
  3. An interest in illumination, both physical and mental.
  4. Astro-physics and the newer astronomical discoveries.

The seventh ray will change the theories of the advanced thinkers of the race into the facts of the future educational systems. Education and the growth of the understanding of illumination in all fields will eventually be regarded as synonymous ideals.

h. The sixth ray taught the meaning of sacrifice, and of this teaching the crucifixion was the outstanding emblem, to the initiates. Philanthropy was the expression of the same teaching, to advanced humanity. The nebulous ideal of simply "being kind" is the same motivation, applied to the unthinking masses.

The seventh ray will bring to the consciousness of the coming initiates the concept of group service and sacrifice. This will inaugurate the age of the "divine service". The vision of the giving of the individual in sacrifice and service, within the group and to the group ideal, will be the goal of the masses of advanced thinkers in the New Age, whilst for the rest of humanity, brotherhood will be the keynote of their endeavour. These words have a wider connotation and significance than the thinkers of today can know and understand.

i. The sixth ray promoted the growth of the spirit of individualism. Groups exist but they are groups of individuals gathered around an individual.

The seventh ray will foster the group spirit, and the rhythm of the group, the objectives of the group, and the ritual-working of the group will be the basic phenomena.

j. The sixth ray influence conveyed to men the ability to recognise the historical Christ, and to evolve the structure of the Christian faith, coloured by a vision of a great Son of Love, but qualified by an excessive militancy and separativeness, based on a narrow idealism.

The seventh ray will convey to man the power to recognise the cosmic Christ, and to produce that future scientific religion of *Light* which will enable man to fulfill the command of the historical Christ to permit his light to shine forth.

k. The sixth ray produced the great idealistic religions with their vision and their necessary narrowness—a narrowness that is needed to safeguard infant souls.

The seventh ray will release the developed souls from the nursery stage and inaugurate that scientific understanding of the divine purpose which will foster the coming religious synthesis.

1. The effect of the sixth ray influence has been to foster the separative instincts—dogmatic religion, scientific factual accuracy, schools of thought with their doctrinal barriers and exclusiveness, and the cult of patriotism.

The seventh ray will prepare the way for the recognition of the wider issues which will materialise as the new world religion which will emphasise unity but bar out uniformity; it will prepare for that scientific technique which will demonstrate the universal light that every form veils and hides, and for that internationalism which will express itself as practical brotherhood and as peace and goodwill between the peoples.

I could continue emphasising these relations, but I have enumerated enough to show the beauty of the preparation made by the sixth great Lord of Idealism for the work of the seventh Lord of Ceremonial.

EPI 357-63

Another factor enters now—a factor that varies somewhat according to the need of the period. All cycles are not as fundamentally important. The periods in a cycle that are of real moment are the termini, and those where overlapping and merging occur. They demonstrate on the physical plane in great revolutions, gigantic cataclysms, and fundamental upheavals in all three departments of the Hierarchy—the department of the World Teacher, that of the Head of a root-race and that of the Ruler of civilisation or of force. At the points of merging in a cycle, cross-currents are found, and all the system seems to be in a chaotic condition. The middle part of a cycle, where the incoming vibration is stabilised and the old has passed away, manifests in a period of calm and apparent equilibrium.

At no time in the history of the race has this been better shown than in the present half century. The sixth Ray of Devotion passes away and the Ray of Ceremonial Law enters and with that entering comes a swinging into prominence of the outstanding features and faculties of the department of force and activity, the synthesis, forget not, of the four minor rays. Therefore you have the fighting for ideals and the devoted adherence to a cause, as demonstrated under the ray of the Master Jesus; therefore the clashing in every field of endeavour of the idealists (right or wrong) and their bitter warfare. What was the world war but the culmination of two opposing ideals, fighting it out on the physical plane?—it was an instance of the force of the sixth ray. Now will come, as the sixth ray passes out, a gradual cessation of the clashing, and the gradual domination of organisation, rule and order under the sway of the incoming force, that of the ray of the Master R—. Out of the present turbulence will arise the ordered and organised form of the new world. Gradually the new rhythm will impose itself on the disorganised communities of men, and instead of social chaos as now, you will have social order and rule; instead of the religious differences and the differentiated sects of the many so-called religions, you will have religious expression itself regulated into form and all ordered by law; instead of economic and political strain and stress will be seen the harmonious working of the system under certain fundamental forms; all will be dominated by ceremonial with the inner results aimed at by the Hierarchy gradually taking shape. Forget not that in the apotheosis of law and order and their resultant forms and limitations lies, towards the close (I choose my words with deliberation), a fresh period of chaos, and the escape of

Transformation from a Sixth to a Seventh Ray Cycle   27

the imprisoned life from even those limitations, bearing with it the imparted faculty and the essence of the development aimed at by the Logos of the seventh ray.

Such is the situation from time to time down through the ages. Each ray sweeps into power, bearing its own incarnating Spirits to whom the period marks a point of least resistance comparatively. They contact six other types of force in the worlds and six other groups of beings who must be impressed by that force and be carried forward in its sweep towards the universal goal. Such is also the specific situation in the period in which you live, a period wherein the seventh Logos of Ceremonial Law and Order seeks to straighten out the temporary chaos, and aims at the reduction within limits of the life escaping from the old and worn-out forms. The new forms are needed now and will be adequate. It is only after the middle period in a new cycle that limitation will again be felt and the attempt to escape be started anew.

Therefore the wise teacher at this time considers the situation and weighs the effect of the incoming ray on the spirits in incarnation. Here, therefore, you have a third ray and its bearing to be considered in the assigning of meditation. Complex you feel the task to be? Fortunately the Hall of Wisdom equips its graduates for the task.

At this particular period the aspect of the Form in meditation (whether meditation based principally on the egoic ray or on the personality ray) will be much developed. You can look to see very definite forms built up and assigned, both to individuals and to groups, resulting in an increase of white magic, and the consequent resultant, on the physical plane, of law and order. The coming period of reconstruction goes forward in line with the ray, and its ultimate success and achievement is more nearly possible than perhaps is looked for. The Great Lord comes in under the law and naught can stop His approach.

Just now the great need of the time is for those who understand the law and can work with it. Now is the opportunity, too, for the development of that principle and the training of people in the helping of the world.

The minor Rays of Harmony and Science respond quickly to this seventh influence; by that statement I mean that their monads are easily influenced in this direction. The monads of the sixth Ray of Devotion find conformity more difficult, until nearing the point of synthesis. The monads of the first and second rays find in this ray a field of expression. First ray monads have a direct link with this ray and seek to wield the law through power, whilst second ray monads, being the synthetic type, guide and rule through love.

LOM 40-43

Besides regarding the rays as the channels through which all being flows, we must recognise them as influences operating on the world in turn. Each ray has its period of greatest influence, to which all are subject to a considerable extent, not merely those belonging by nature to that particular ray, but those on all the other rays as well. The long period of influence of each is divided into seven stages, each of which is qualified by the influence of the greater ray period, being intensified when its own sub-ray period is reached (i.e., the sixth ray influence is greatest during the period of the sixth sub-ray). We must carefully note that the term "sub-ray" is used merely for convenience to designate the shorter period of influence, not as indicating any difference in the nature of the ray.

We are told that the dominant ray at the present time, though passing out, is the sixth, the Ray of Devotion, and that this ray was already in operation before the dawn of Christianity; also that the seventh sub-ray became the modifying influence about seventy-five years ago (1860), and of course will continue as such. The first outcome of this seventh sub-ray influence was the Ecumenical Council at Rome (1870), with its declaration of Papal Infallibility. The Tractarian Movement in England started at the same time, whilst the progress of the seventh sub-ray influence, still going on, is marked by the steady increase of ritualism and sacerdotalism in the various churches, and even in the church of Rome there has been a distinct tightening of priestly authority in all matters of dogma and practice. So much for its influence on religious thought; its other aspects will be considered later.

We have also been told that the religious revival under Wesley and Whitfield in England was under the sixth sub-ray, and I think we are justified in drawing the inference that the rise of Molinos and the Quietists in Spain and Central Europe, and of St. Martin and his band of spiritual philosophers in France and elsewhere, may have also marked the progress of the same period, during which the Ray of Devotion was accentuated by its own sixth sub-ray.

With these few isolated facts before us we may perhaps conclude that the time during which each sub-ray exerts its modifying influence is between one hundred and fifty and two hundred years.

We do not know how often (perhaps seven times?) the sub-rays are repeated successively within the cycle of the great ray. It must manifestly be more than once, seeing that the great sixth ray was operating before the rise of Christianity. It is also apparent that Buddhism cannot have been, as was at one time thought, the last outcome of the great second ray period, for the interval between the rise of Buddhism and that of Christianity was only five hundred years. It seems probable that Buddhism arose under the influence of the second sub-ray of the great sixth ray period. In attempting to trace back the influence which was the last outcome of the sub-rays, 5.4.3.2. and 1, it has been suggested that this period of the Alchemists and Rosicrucians may have been dominated by the fifth sub-ray; the epoch of the Flagellants and other fanatical enthusiasts who practised self-torture and mutilation was influenced by the fourth sub-ray; and the time when astrology was widely practised as representing the third sub-ray; while the earlier epoch of the Gnostics may have been the outcome of the second sub-ray. But these are only conjectures, and while the last named is possible, there can be no such correspondence of time in the previous cases, as the Alchemists, Flagellants, and Astrologers were all more or less contemporary during the Middle Ages.

EPI 164-66

...It remains for us now to consider the energy of the two minor rays, the sixth and the seventh, which are in many ways of more immediate moment to the masses and of a tremendous effectiveness. One is of moment because of its pronounced hold and because of the crystallisation it has produced particularly in the world of thought, and the other because its hold and its power, its influence and its effects will be of an increasing momentum. One is potent in producing the necessity for the present chaos; the other is potential and holds in its activity the seeds of the future.

This is a fact of great interest and of really practical import. It takes us, moreover, into the realm of prevision. I would have you remember, at this point, that no prevision is divorced entirely from the past but that there must always be the seed of truth. The Law of Cause and Effect holds good eternally and particularly so in the realm of spiritual insight (so rapidly developing at this time) which enables the seer to see the future as it may be and to forecast coming eventualities. There are several ways in which such prevision can—during the next three centuries—be developed in the race of men:

Transformation from a Sixth to a Seventh Ray Cycle 31

1. Through the development of soul contact among the advanced members of the race. This contact will relate soul knowledge with brain impression and, if the meditating factor of the mind is duly trained and controlled, there will be a correct foreknowledge of individual destiny and of coming events.

2. Through the development of the science of astrology—a science which is, as yet, in its infancy and which is based on so many uncertain factors that it is difficult for a student to arrive at those true indications which will truly present the future. Character indications and small personality happenings can frequently and correctly be deduced but the general subject remains until today much too nebulous for certitude. I will later deal with this matter and will indicate the lines along which future investigation should proceed.

3. Through the recurrence of "soothsaying" and the reappearance of those ancient "informers of the race" who, in Roman times, were called "sibyls". These mediums (for such they were) will be trained by the workers upon the seventh ray to speak under inspiration from the Hierarchy Whose foreknowledge extends far ahead into the future, but does not extend beyond two thousand years. These mediums will, however, only be used under direction, after careful training and only twice a year at the May and June Full Moon rituals.

As to the prevision with which I shall deal, unorthodox as it may appear to be to some of you, it will be based upon two factors: First of all, the logical indications to be gathered from past and present events which condition the immediate future and which must inevitably lead to definite and tangible happenings. Any deep student of human affairs could follow the same line of reasoning and come to approximately the same conclusions, *provided* he loved his fellowmen enough to see them truly as they were and allow, consequently, for the appearance of the unexpected. And, secondly, what I may say to you is based on a knowledge of the ray influences which are at this time so powerfully and effectively affecting humanity and its coming civilisation and culture.

I would ask you, therefore, to read what I have to say with an open mind; I would beg you to relate my words to present world conditions and to see, emerging from the realms of subjectivity, those forces and potencies which are directly changing the current of men's thoughts, which are moulding their ideas, and incidentally altering the face of the earth and the policies of nations.

As you know, there are at this time, two minor rays (which are rays of attribute) affecting powerfully the destiny of mankind. These are the sixth Ray of Abstract Devotion or Idealism and the seventh Ray of Ceremonial Magic or Organisation. The sixth ray began to pass out of manifestation in 1625 after a long period of influence, whilst the seventh Ray of Ceremonial Order began to come into manifestation in 1675. There are three points to be remembered in connection with these two rays and their effects upon the race of men. (I am not here dealing with their effects upon the other kingdoms in nature.)

1. The sixth ray is, as you know, the most powerful in manifestation at this time and a very large number of people are responsive to its influence. It is still the line of least resistance for the majority, particularly in the Aryan race, for the reason that when in process of time and through evolution the influence of a ray has become potent, it is groups that are primarily affected and not just individuals. A rhythm and a momentum is then set up which lasts a long time and which gains power through the very force of organised numbers. This truth will emerge more clearly as we proceed with

our studies. Suffice it to say that the sixth ray people are the reactionaries, the conservatives, the die-hards and the fanatics, who hold on to all that is of the past and whose influence is potent to hinder the progress of humanity into the new age. Their name is legion. They provide, however, a needed balance and are responsible for a steadying process which is much needed in the world at this time.

2. The seventh ray is steadily gaining momentum and has for a long time been stimulating and enhancing the activity of all fifth ray nations. If you bear in mind that one of the major objectives of seventh ray energy is to bring together and to relate spirit and matter and also substance and form (note this distinction) you can see for yourself that the work of science is closely connected with this endeavour and that the creation of the new forms will definitely be the result of a working interaction between the rulers of the fifth, the second and the seventh rays, aided by the help—on demand—of the ruler of the first ray. A large number of seventh ray egos or souls and also of men and women with seventh ray personalities are coming into incarnation now, and to them is committed the task of organising the activities of the new era and of ending the old methods of life and the old crystallised attitudes to life, to death, to leisure, and to the population.

3. The result of the increasing flow of seventh ray energy plus the decreasing influence of the sixth ray—which shows itself as a pronounced crystallisation of the standardised and accepted forms of belief, religious, social and philosophic—is to throw the millions of people who do not respond to either of the above influences through egoic or personality relation, into a state of bewilderment. They feel entirely lost, are gripped by the idea that life holds for them no desirable future, all

that they have learnt to cherish and to hold dear is rapidly failing.

These three groups of people, influenced by the sixth and seventh rays or who are bewildered by the impact of forces generated by those rays, are those who must together, with understanding and clear vision, bring order out of the present chaos. They must materialise those new and desirable conditions which will conform to the subjective pattern in the minds of the illumined people of the world and to the spiritual plan as it exists in the consciousness of the members of the Hierarchy. The new age with its peculiar civilisation and culture will be brought into manifestation through the collaboration of the well-intentioned many, responsive increasingly to the good of the whole and not of the individual; they are the idealistic but practical thinkers, influenced by the pattern of things to come and the world disciples, impressed by the plans and under the instruction of the Hierarchy which is directing and controlling all.

It is with these three groups of people and with the work upon which they are engaged that any prevision I may evidence will consistently deal. All changes in connection with the human family, the fourth kingdom in nature, are always dependent on three factors:

1. Those outer physical events which are definitely "acts of God" and over which no human being has the slightest authority.

2. The activity of human beings themselves, working on all the different rays but in any given time and in any particular period conditioned by:

    a. The preponderance of egos to be found on any particular ray. There are a very large number of second ray egos in incarnation today and their work and their lives will facilitate the coming Great Approach.

b. The nature and the quality of the predominating personality rays of the majority. At this time there are a vast number of souls in incarnation whose personality rays are either the sixth or the third. They condition the coming civilisation outstandingly including all educational and financial enterprises, just as the influence of those who have soul contact and can express soul quality condition and determine the current culture.

c. The activity of the fifth principle, that of the mind. This mind principle is peculiarly active today in a broad and general sense. If I might put it symbolically the vertical activity of the mind which has affected individuals everywhere down the ages has always produced the mental guides, the directors and the leaders of humanity. Today, the *horizontal activity* of the mind, embracing huge masses of the populace and sometimes entire nations and races, can everywhere be seen and this must lead inevitably to events and effects hitherto unvisioned and impossible.

3. The influence of the outgoing and the incoming rays at any time. You have often been told that these events—for the emergence or disappearance of a ray influence is an event in time—are a matter of slow development, are psychic in nature, and are governed by law. The length of time in which a ray appears, manifests and does its work and finally disappears is one of the secrets of initiation, but—as time elapses and the nature of time itself is better understood—the period and the time equation of the minor rays of attribute will be established but that time is not yet, although the intense interest taken today in the phenomena of time indicates a growing awareness of the problem itself and of the need for understanding the relation of time, both to space and to event. It will be realised before

long that time is entirely a brain event; a study of the sense of speed as registered by the brain, plus the capacity or incapacity of a human being to express this speed, will, when properly approached, reveal much that today remains a mystery.

At this time, the whole world is embroiled in the chaos and the turmoil incident upon the clashing of the forces of the sixth and the seventh rays. As one ray passes out and another comes into manifestation and their impact upon the earth and upon all the forms in all the kingdoms of nature has reached the point where the two influences are equalised, then a definite point of crisis is reached. This is what has occurred today, and humanity, subjected to two types or forms of energy, is thrown "off centre" and hence the intense difficulty and tension of the present world period. The cause of this is not only the impact of the two types of energy, beating upon the forms of life with equal force, but also that the energy of humanity itself (which is a combination of the fourth and fifth rays) is swept into the conflict. To this must also be added the energy of the animal kingdom (again a combination of the energies of the third, fifth and sixth rays) for this governs the animal or physical form of every human being. You have, therefore, a meeting of many conflicting forces and the world Arjuna is faced with a stupendous battle—one that is recurrent and cyclic but which will, in this particular era, prove a decisive and determining factor in the age old conflict between material domination and spiritual control. The forces playing upon the planet at this time are of supreme importance. If you will bear in mind that the sixth ray works through and controls the solar plexus (being closely related to the astral plane, the sixth level of awareness) and that the seventh ray controls the sacral centre, you will see why there is so much emotion, so much idealism and so much desire mixed up in connection with the world conflict and why also—apart from the storms in the political arena and the religious field—that sex and its various problems has reached a point of interest in the human consciousness where a solution of these difficulties, a fresh understanding of the underlying implications and a frank dealing with the situation is inevitable and immediate.

DN 26-34

I have stated that the incoming seventh ray plays through the planetary sacral centre, and then through the sacral centre of every human being. Because of this, we can look for the anticipated developments in that human function which we designate the sex function. We shall see consequent changes in the attitude of man towards this most difficult problem....

EPI 268

One point I would like here to bring to your attention and that is that the two great groups of divine agents—the Great White Brotherhood and the Lodge of Materialistic Forces—are both of them seeking to divert these energies into channels which will further the ends for which they work and for which they were formed and exist. Therefore, I would ask you to remember that behind all the outer events are these two directing agencies. You have, as a consequence:

1. Two groups of advanced Minds, both groups equally illumined by the light of the intellect, and both of them formulating clearly their objectives, but differing in their direction and their emphasis. One group, under the divine plan, works with the form aspect entirely, and in this group the light of love and of selflessness is absent. The other group is working entirely with the soul or the consciousness aspect, and in this group the doctrine of the heart and the law of love control.

In this connection, the two groups are working in opposition, therefore, upon the mental plane.

2. The plans, which embody these two differing ideals and objectives, are next carried down on to the astral plane, and thus into the world of desire. The lines of demarcation remain ever entirely clear as far as the workers in these two groups are concerned, but are not so clear where ordinary human beings and the world disciples and initiates are concerned. There is much chaos on the plane of desire, and the world Arjuna is today sitting in bewilderment between the two opposing forces or camps, recognising his relationship both to form and to soul and at the same time wondering where his duty lies. His point in evolution determines his problem.

Thus the two groups are working in opposition upon the plane of desire.

3. The materialising of the plans of these two groups of illumined minds proceeds steadily under the differing laws of their being—the laws of form life and the laws of spiritual living. In this initial stage and whilst the battle is being fought out in the realm of desire (for that is where the major conflict is being waged, and all that is happening upon the physical plane is only a reflection of an inner conflict) the forces of these two groups, working with the energies of the sixth and seventh rays, have brought about in the field of physical living, a state of complete cataclysm. The economic situation and the religious hatreds are the two major instruments. This is a subject upon which you would do well to ponder.

Consequently, you have two groups, two objectives, two great formulated ideals, two streams of active energy and two rays predominantly in conflict, thus producing the differing ideologies. The result of this dualism is the external chaos, the differentiation of the two group ideals into the many human experiments, and the resultant ranging of the entire human family under many banners, which testify to the various viewpoints in the many fields of thought—political, religious, economic, social, educational and philosophical. The result of all this conflict is, I would tell you, definitely good, and it demonstrates the steady achievement of the Great White Lodge. The consciousness of humanity has been definitely expanded and the whole world of men at this time is thinking. This is a totally new phenomenon and a fresh experience in the life of the human soul. The first result of all the turmoil has been to shift the focus of human attention on to the mental plane and thereby nearer to the sources of light and love.

It is right here and in connection with this eventful change of focus that the world disciples can shoulder responsibility and proceed to active work. When I here speak of disciples, I am using the term in connection with all who aspire to true humanity, to brotherhood, and to the living expression of the higher and spiritual values. I am not using it altogether in the technical sense, which involves a recognised relation to the Hierarchy through the grades of probationary or accepted discipleship, though these are included in my thought. I refer to all aspirants and to all who have any sense of true values and an urge to meet the world's need.

To understand a little the problem involved and the differing modes of work which characterise those who worked in the past under the influence of the sixth ray and those who are learning to work under the influence of the incoming seventh ray, it might be helpful if we compared very briefly the two systems of activity. I would ask you to remember that both systems and modes of work are equally right in their time and place, but that the modern disciple should be discarding the old methods and steadily learning to employ the new and more modern and effective modes of work. This he must learn to do optimistically and with assurance, knowing that the benefits and the experience gained under the sixth ray system of discipline is still his most precious possession because it has been transmuted from method and mode into characteristics and established habits. It is the new ways of working and the new forces and objectives which the disciple of this present era has to master; he must do this relying upon the lessons learnt in the past and must base his new structure of truth upon the foundations and the stabilised orientations, which must now be established.

The first step for the sincere aspirant is at this point to stop for a moment to enquire and discover whether he is working primarily under the sixth ray impulse or the seventh ray influence. I use these words "impulse and influence" deliberately because they describe the general effect of the two functioning energies. Upon one thing all disciples and aspirants can rely and this is the basic and enduring effect of all the sixth ray potencies which have been established during the past two thousand years. These must be counted upon, offset and understood and the newer influence must then be studied, the newer methods investigated and mastered, and the new ideas and idealisms must be brought through into objectivity and so expressed in a new way. Only thus can the new civilisation and culture be wisely and sanely produced and the foundations laid for the development of the human family along right lines during the coming era. It will be of value, therefore, to compare the old and the new ways of discipline and of training, of attribute and quality, and of method and objectives.

Let us take the sixth ray methods of activity and its major characteristics first of all. They are, for us, the most familiar and can be rapidly considered, enabling us to pass

Transformation from a Sixth to a Seventh Ray Cycle 41

on to the new ways of demonstrating and discovering the ancient wisdom, and to the comprehension of the fresh modes of working which will give new vitality to the work of the Hierarchy upon the physical plane.

The outstanding characteristic of the disciple and the aspirant under the old regime was *devotion*. The race had, of necessity, to achieve a different and right orientation to the world of spiritual values, and hence the effort of the Hierarchy during the past twenty centuries was to lay the emphasis upon the realm of religious values. The world religions have held the centre of the stage for several thousand years in an effort to make humanity seek one-pointedly for the soul and thus prepare itself for the emergence of the fifth kingdom in nature. This is slated (if I might use such a specialised word) to come into manifestation during the imminent Aquarian age; this age will be predominantly the age of worldwide discipleship, leading later to the age of universal initiation in Capricornian times. Therefore the great world religions have held authoritative sway for a very long time; their peculiar tenets, adapted to a specific nation, race or time, embodied some truth through the medium of some particular teacher who attracted to himself individuals throughout the world who were spiritually minded, because he expressed for them the highest goal towards which they could possibly strive. All the world religions have been thus built around an embodied Idea, Who, in His Own Person, expressed the immediate ideal of the time and age. He demonstrated certain divine attributes and concepts which it was necessary to present to the vision of the sons of men as their possible and immediate goal. In these manifestations—as I have earlier pointed out—the sixth ray influence can easily be seen. When, however, an individual sixth ray influence can be noted in an era wherein the sixth ray is uniquely active, then the reason for the potency of the religious idea, as expressed in theological dogma and doctrine and the universal authority of the Churches can be seen.

This orientation of man to the world of higher values has been the main objective of the Piscean age which is ending now and of the sixth ray influence which is so rapidly passing out. Though there has never been a time when this basic orientation has not been going steadily forward, it is of value to bear in mind that during the past two thousand years a much higher, rarer and more difficult process of orientation has been held before the race and for the following reason. The fourth kingdom in nature has been definitely attracted upwards towards the emerging fifth kingdom and this has made necessary also the shift of attention away from the three worlds of human endeavour and expression into the higher world of soul consciousness. It has necessitated likewise the refocussing of the instinctual and intellectual attention which are the main factors in the unfoldment of divine awareness. This awareness can be instinctual, intellectual and therefore human, and also spiritual. But all three are equally divine, which is a point oft forgotten.

The second objective of the sixth ray disciple or of the man who is emerging out of the sixth ray influence but is still conditioned by it (being a representative human being from the current evolutionary angle) has been the unfolding of the "capacity for abstraction", as it has been called. The outstanding quality of our day and period, as a result of transmuting human quality and character in and through its disciples, has been the expression of the idealistic nature of man, or of his instinctual response to the higher intuitional values. In the past, highly developed but rare people have here and there demonstrated this power to abstract the consciousness from the material or form side of life and to focus it upon the ideal and upon the formless expression of living truth. Today, whole masses of people and entire nations are regimented to certain forms of idealism and can and do appreciate ideas, formulated into ideals. Thus again the success of the evolutionary process can be seen and the work of the Hierarchy, as it endeavours to expand human consciousness, can be demonstrated to be effective.

Because of the potency of the sixth ray activity, owing to the long period wherein it has been expressing itself, the reaction of the average human being is one of an intense devotion to his own particular ideal, plus the effort, fanatically, to impose his idealistic dream (for that is all it potentially is) upon his fellowmen and to do so in such a form that unfortunately the original idea is lost, the primal ideal is destroyed and the devotee becomes much more occupied by the method of applying his ideal than by the ideal itself. Thus the idea is lost in the ideal and the ideal, in its turn, in the method of its application. The man becomes the devotee of an ideal which may or may not be embodied in an individual expression; this controls his thoughts, fore-ordains his activities and leads him frequently to merciless excesses in the interest of his peculiar and formulated idea.

Under the immediate expression of the sixth ray, the divine principle of desire has shifted potently away from the desire for material form into the realm of higher desire. Though materialism is still rampant, there are few people who are not animated by certain definite idealistic aspirations for which they are ready, when needed, to make sacrifices. This is a relatively new phenomenon and one that should be carefully noted. Down the ages, great sons of God have ever been ready to die for an idea; today, whole masses of men are equally ready and have done so, whether it is the idea of a superhuman state, empire or nation, or some response to a major world need, or some potent adherence to some current ideology. This indicates phenomenal racial achievement and the pronounced success of the Hierarchy to shift human attention into the world from whence ideas emerge and on to the higher and the less material values.

The instinct which has characterised this passing sixth ray period and which has been noticeably fostered under its influence is that of taste—taste in food, in human intercourse, in colour, in form, in art and architecture and in all branches of human knowledge. This discriminating taste has reached a relatively high stage of development during the past two thousand years and "good taste" is a highly cherished mass virtue and objective today. This is a totally new thing and one which has been hitherto the prerogative of the highly cultured few. Ponder on this. It connotes evolutionary achievement. For the disciples of the world, this sense of taste has to be transmuted into its higher correspondence—a discriminating sense of values. Hence the clear emphasis laid in all textbooks on discipleship upon the need to develop *discrimination.* Desire—taste—discrimination; these are the values, under the sixth ray, for all evolutionary unfoldment and peculiarly the goal of all disciples.

The methods whereby the activity of the sixth ray and its objectives have been imposed upon the race are three in number:

1. The development of instinct. This is followed by intelligently recognised desire and thus there is a steady expansion of requirements, of realisation and then of reorientation.

2. The consequent stimulation of the human consciousness towards expansion, leading finally to spiritual aspiration.

3. The reflection of reality in the mind consciousness fol-

Transformation from a Sixth to a Seventh Ray Cycle   45

lows next and this is sensed, demanded and sought through the medium of group work.

The apparatus of the human being, which is the mechanism whereby the soul contacts the three worlds which would be otherwise (under the present plan) sealed and hidden to the experience and experiment of the soul, has been more acutely sensitised and developed during the past two thousand years than in any previous period of ten thousand years. The reason for this is that the mind of man has been consciously aiding in the process of coordinating the instincts and transmuting instinctual reaction, translating it into intelligent perception. In the case of the world disciples, this process has been carried forward into the next stage of unfoldment to which we give the name of intuitional knowledge. The counterparts of the five senses and their higher correspondences upon the subtler planes are being rapidly unfolded, organised and recognised and it is by means of these inner senses that spiritual discovery becomes possible as well as the more familiar psychic discoveries. In the three phases:

a. Instinct to aspiration
b. Stimulation of divine desire
c. The reflection of reality

you have the history of the activity of the sixth ray and of its relation during the past few centuries to its major field of expression, the astral plane.

We can now proceed to consider the seventh ray in its relation to the present situation in just the same way as we considered the sixth ray. Through doing this, there will unfold in your consciousness an idea of the developing process and of the emerging events and of the imminent happenings which may logically be expected. There are, as you may realise, two ways in which any particular ray may be considered. It can be studied, first of all, from the angle of energy which is ever coming into relation with other energies and forces, producing through their meeting and frequent conflict a situation entirely different and changed from that which existed prior to the contact. The stages of this import might be covered briefly by the following words: Contact, conflict, adjustment, equilibrium (a form of stalemate or static condition such as was arrived at during the 19th century), absorption and the final disappearance of the weaker outgoing energy. The conclusion is always inevitable for it is not the rays themselves which are in conflict but the substance and the forms which are implicated during the period. Secondly: the quality of the ray can be considered. This is in reality the expression of its soul and intrinsic nature, which—impinging upon the condition existing when the ray comes into manifestation—definitely does three things:

1. Changes the nature of the civilisation and the culture of humanity in any given period. It is this force which the Hierarchy utilises when any meeting of the ray energies takes place. The culture is first changed, because *all basic quality changes* work ever from above downwards, and it is the intelligentsia who are at first sensitive to the incoming differences. Form changes then automatically reverse the process. It is thus that points of juncture inevitably occur throughout the evolutionary process. When the scientists concerned with the theory and processes of evolution accept and study the ray procedure, definite changes in attitude and a closer approach to the truth will at once appear. This concept also lies behind the teaching which I have given anent the Great Approaches which must take place (and can take place very shortly) between the fourth and the fifth kingdoms in nature. Of the fifth kingdom, the Hierarchy is the dynamic and living nucleus.

2. Changes in the other kingdoms in nature, producing a different quality in the manifestation of the soul of any

Transformation from a Sixth to a Seventh Ray Cycle

kingdom (for they all differ in soul quality) and consequently changes in the form aspect as well.

3. Changes in the type of egos or souls which will take incarnation during any particular ray period. By this I mean that just as during the age which is now coming to an end, the bulk of the incarnating souls were predominantly sixth ray in quality, so we can look for an increasing number of seventh ray egos now to appear. The furtherance of the coming seventh ray civilisation of synthesis, fusion, and of increased soul expression, and the development of the new stage into which the white magic of the Hierarchy is entering is, therefore, inevitable and for this stage there should be definite preparation and training.

The powers of the magical age are many and one of the reasons why the seventh ray is now making its appearance is that, owing to the rapid perfecting and integration of the human personality, the higher integration between soul and personality is today more possible and more easily accomplished than ever before. The new forms, through which that much desired consummation can be effected, must be consequently gradually and scientifically developed. This, as you may well conceive, will be achieved through the intensification of the forces, functioning through the etheric body, through the coordination of the seven major centres, and the establishing of their rhythmic relationship. The seventh ray governs predominantly upon the etheric levels of the physical plane. It does not govern the dense physical form which is under the control of the third ray. It is the vital or the etheric body which is responsive to and developed by the incoming seventh ray influences.

In considering the methods whereby the seventh ray purposes are achieved, I would like to point out that it is in this part of our discussion that I am limited and handicapped by language, because we are dealing with that which is new and, therefore, not as yet to be truly comprehended, and with those developments which will be eventually brought about by means of a true and scientific magic. This new magic will have no more relation to the crude attempts and oft ridiculous undertakings of the magicians, alchemists and performers of the past than c-a-t, cat, has to an algebraical formula. I would remind you also that in that home of ancient magic which you call Egypt, the magical work there performed was definitely concentrated upon the producing of physical effects and material results, and that the focus of the attention of the magician of the day can be seen in the stupendous production of those ancient and gigantic forms, standing silent and still in their pristine magnificence, which today call for the attention of archeologists and travellers; the forms of lesser magic which they produced were dedicated to the magical protection of the physical form and allied matters. In later days, we have the appearance of alchemy in its many forms plus its search for the Philosopher's Stone and the teaching as to the three basic mineral elements. They were driven esoterically and from the subjective side of life to search for that which could unify the three lower physical levels and this is in its nature deeply symbolic of racial unfoldment. These levels symbolise the integrated man—physical, astral and mental. When to these elements the Philosopher's Stone is added and has done its magical work, then you have the symbolic representation of the control by the soul of the four higher levels of the physical plane, the etheric or energy levels. Of this desirable consummation, the Philosopher's Stone is the emblem. I said "emblem", and I did not say "symbol". A symbol is an outer and visible sign of an inner and spiritual reality, carried out into expression upon the physical plane by the force of the inner embodied life. An emblem is man's formulation of a concept, created by man and embodying for him the truth as he sees it and understands it. A symbol is ever greater in its implications than is an emblem.

The etheric levels are also the field of expression for the soul, whether it is the human soul or the soul as an expression of the higher triad, the monadic life. I wonder whether any of you have the faintest idea what will happen to humanity when the inner subjective reality, functioning through the etheric body and pouring its forces unimpeded through the centres in that body, will have made its major controlling integration with the dense physical apparatus, reducing it to complete submission as a result of the higher integration, consummated between soul and personality.

We are, therefore, at a most interesting and crucial period in racial and planetary history—a period unlike any which has preceded it and for the reason that the evolutionary process has been definitely successful in spite of all failures, mistakes, and delays; of these latter there have been many owing to the refusal (curious and difficult to understand in your eyes) of the Energies, concentrated at Shamballa, to impose the force of will on matter and on form until such time as this can be done with the cooperation of the human family. This has never been possible hitherto, owing to the unpreparedness of man for the task and his ignorance as to the Plan. The Lord of Shamballa and His Helpers have had to wait until at least the dim outlines of the Plan had penetrated through into the consciousness of the race; this is beginning to happen with increasing frequency, and from day to day more and more intelligent men and women are coming (or are being brought) into touch with the emerging ideas of the Hierarchy. We can look, therefore, for the steady appearance, gradually and cautiously applied, of the will energy of the highest centre (Shamballa) which is to be found upon our planet. This centre corresponds to the monadic centre which makes its power felt in the consciousness of the disciple who is ready for the third initiation. Once the second initiation has been taken, the watching Hierarchy can begin to note the constant reorientation of the soul towards the monad, and the attractive power of that highest aspect over the initiate. Today, so many members of the human family—in incarnation or out of incarnation—have taken the first two initiations that the attention of Shamballa is being increasingly turned to humanity, via the Hierarchy, whilst simultaneously the thoughts of men are being turned to the Plan, to the use of the will in direction and guidance, and to the nature of dynamic force. The quality, for instance, of the explosive and dynamic nature of war in this century is indicative of this, for the will energy in one of its aspects is an expression of death and destruction; the first ray is the ray of the destroyer. What can, therefore, be seen occurring is the effect of the Shamballa force upon the forms in nature, due to the misuse of the incoming energy by man. War in the past, speaking generally and esoterically, has been based consistently upon the attractive power of possessions and this has led to the aggressive and grasping character of the motives which have led to war. Gradually there has been a change coming about and war has lately been founded upon somewhat higher motives and the acquisition of more land and territorial possessions has not been the true and the main motive. War has been prompted by economic necessity, or it has been in the nature of the imposition of the will of some nation or group of nations and their desire to impose some ideology or other upon some nation or to rid itself of a worn out system of thought, of government, of religious dogma which is holding back racial development. This is being now consciously done and is an expression of the

Shamballa or will force and is not so definitely the desire force of the past.

The seventh ray is one of the direct lines along which this first ray energy can travel and here again is another reason for its appearance at this time, because, in the releasing of the life into the new and improved forms, the old ways of living, of culture and of civilization have to be destroyed or modified. This is, all of it, the work of the first Ray of Will expressing itself predominantly at this present time through the seventh Ray of Organisation and Relationship.

When we studied the sixth ray, we considered first of all the effect of the ray upon the work and training, the life and the plans of the disciple, conditioning as it inevitably must his activities and life output. Then we considered the motivating principle of desire in this connection and finally touched upon the three modes of the prevalent ray activity. Let us follow the same procedure now, thus gaining some idea of the relationship between the sixth and the seventh rays and the manner in which the potency of the sixth ray has prepared humanity for the imminent happenings with which it is faced.

What I have now to say will not be followed with ease or with due appreciation by the sixth ray disciple, because the methods employed by Those Who are handling and directing the new energies are not comprehensible by him, grounded as he is in the methods of the past; hence the appearance of fundamentalist schools, found in every field of thought—religious, political and even scientific. Again, when the sixth ray disciple attempts to use the new incoming energies, they express themselves for him upon the astral plane and the result is astral magic, deepened glamour and pronounced deception. To this fact must be ascribed today the appearance of teachers, claiming to teach magic, to bring about certain magical results, to work with rays of differing colours and to utilise Words of Power, to pronounce decrees and to be repositories of the hitherto unrevealed wishes and secrets of the Masters of the Wisdom. It is all a form of astral glamour, and the contacting upon the astral plane of that which will later precipitate upon earth. But the time is not yet and the hour for such usages has not arrived. The sense of time and the understanding of the correct hour for the carrying out of the Plan in its future detail has not been learnt by these sincere but deluded, people and—focussed as they are upon the astral plane and undeveloped as they are mentally—they misinterpret to themselves and for others that which they there psychically sense. They know far too little and yet believe that they know much. They speak with authority, but it is the authority of the unexpanded mind. The expression of old magical patterns, the digging up of hints and indications of crystallised and worn-out methods from the ancient past is all too prevalent at this time and is responsible for much deception of the masses and consequent mass delusion.

DN 107-22

In this comparative, even if inadequate, study of the old and of the new types of discipleship, one of the problems facing the Hierarchy is how to bring about the necessary changes in technique and method of development which the seventh ray type will require and yet at the same time so condition these changes that there can be smooth process of adjustment and interplay between the Hierarchy and the world aspirants. This adjustment must include the two groups (one at present large and the other still small) of sixth and seventh ray disciples. The problems of the Hierarchy are, of course, no real concern of those who have not achieved liberation and cannot, therefore, look at life through the eyes of those who are no

Transformation from a Sixth to a Seventh Ray Cycle 53

longer held by the forces of the three worlds, but it might serve a useful purpose if disciples occasionally gave some thought to the relation as it exists upon the Masters' side and gave less thought to their own individual and peculiar difficulties.

One of the major characteristics of the seventh ray disciple is his intense practicality. He works upon the physical plane with a constant and steady objective in order to bring about results which will be effective in determining the forms of the coming culture and civilisation; towards the end of the seventh ray cycle he will work equally hard to perpetuate what he has brought about. He wields force in order to build the forms which will meet his requirements and does this more scientifically than do disciples on other rays. The sixth ray devotee is far more abstract and mystical in his work and thought, and seldom has any real understanding of the right relation between form and energy. He thinks almost entirely in terms of quality and pays little attention to the material side of life and the true significance of substance as it produces phenomena. He is apt to regard matter as evil in nature and form as a limitation, and only lays the emphasis upon soul consciousness as of true importance. It is this failure to work intelligently, and I would like to add, lovingly with substance and so bring it into right relation with the dense outer form that has made the last two thousand years produce so disastrously a mismanaged world and which has brought the population of the planet into its present serious condition. The unintelligent work upon the physical plane, carried forward by those influenced by the sixth ray force, has led to a world which is suffering from cleavage in as true a sense as an individual person can suffer from a "split personality". The lines of demarcation between science and religion are a striking instance of this and have been clearly and forcefully drawn. The cleavage to which I refer has been drawn by the churchmen of the past and by no one else; the lines have been determined by the mystics, impractical and visionary, and by the fanatical devotees of some idea who were, nevertheless, unable to see the broad implications and the universal nature of these recognised ideas. I am generalising. There have been many devoted and holy sons of God who have never been guilty of the above stupidities and separative tendencies. At the same time as we recognise this, we must also recognise that orthodox religion has temporarily separated the two great concepts of spirit and matter in their thought and teaching, thereby pushing apart religion and science.

The task of the new age workers is to bring these two apparent opposites together, to demonstrate that spirit and matter are not antagonistic to each other and that throughout the universe there is only spiritual substance, working on and producing the outer tangible forms.

When a form and an activity is what you call evil, it is only so because the motivating energy behind the form and responsible for the activity is wrongly oriented, selfishly impulsed and incorrectly used. Here again the two basic truisms of modern occultism (there are others which will be imparted when these two are mastered and rightly applied) are of importance:

1. Energy follows thought.
2. Right motive creates right action and right forms.

These two statements are of very ancient origin but are as yet but little understood. Hence the first thing which every disciple has to learn is the nature, control and direction of energy; he does this by working with initiating causes, by learning the nature of the realm of causes and by developing the capacity to get behind the effect to the cause which generated or produced it. In the case of the individual disciple and in the preliminary stage of his training, this involves the constant investigation of his motives until he has discovered what they are and has so directed his thought that those motives can, in every case, be depended upon to work automatically and dynamically under soul direction.

The sixth ray disciple, in the majority of cases, carries his work down as far as the astral plane and there lies the focus of his attention, his life, and his thought. Automatically and of necessity, his physical nature responds to the impulse sent from the astral plane, motivated from the mental and—at times—directed by the soul. But the potency of this desire and his determination to see the fruit of his labour has produced much difficulty in the past by arresting the true expression of the originating impulse. It is arrested upon the astral plane. This has been balanced by the cyclic intervention of other ray forces or otherwise the situation would be much worse than it is. The seventh ray disciple will bring the energy which he is wielding right down on to the physical plane, thereby producing integration; and the dualism which characterises it will be that of a centre of energy upon the mental plane and one upon the physical plane. The dualism of the sixth ray worker is that of the pairs of opposites upon the astral plane.

It will be apparent, therefore, that, having established the two points of energy (mental and physical), the next task of the worker in magic will be to produce a synthesis upon the physical plane of the available energies, to concretise them, and invest that which has been constructed with the potency of activity and persistence. The energy thus employed will, in the majority of cases, be of three kinds:

1. The energy of the mind. This will be the dominant controlling energy used during the period of accepted discipleship and until the second initiation.

2. The energy of the soul. This will be wielded, used and creatively employed from the second until the third initiation.
3. The energy of soul and mind, blended and synthesised. This combination is of tremendous potency. After the fourth initiation, this will be augmented by energy coming from the Monad.

I would have you bear in mind that, though all is energy yet at the same time in correct esoteric teaching the higher impulsive activity is called *energy* and that which is conditioned by and swept into activity through its agency is called *force*. The terms are therefore relative and movable. For the bulk of humanity, for instance, astral impulse is the highest energy to which they normally aspire and the forces upon which astral energy plays will then be the etheric and physical forces. Higher energies may intermittently control, but as a general rule the life incentive or impulse is astral, and this can either be called desire or aspiration, according to the objective. The latter may simply be mental ambition or desire for power and the term "aspiration" should not be confined only to so-called religious impulses, mystical longings and the demand for liberation.

The seventh ray disciple works consciously by means of certain laws, which are the laws governing form and its relation to spirit or life. In *A Treatise on Cosmic Fire*, I gave you the three major laws of the solar system and the seven subsidiary laws through which these three express themselves: I gave you also indications as to the laws which govern group work. You must remember that disciples upon different rays will wield these laws according to the quality of their ray impulses (I am handicapped here for words which are appropriate), interpreting them in terms of their specific life obligation or dharma and producing the desired results through the medium of differing ray techniques, conforming always, however, to the inevitability of the results wrought by the energies which they have released to play upon forces under the laws of their being. The sixth ray disciple, working with the laws of nature and of the soul, will qualify his results and produce his creative forms upon the astral plane; he has consequently to learn frequently to work through a seventh ray personality for several lives (either before or after achieving discipleship) before he will be able to bring through on to the physical plane his dream and his vision. The seventh ray disciple has no such problem. By his knowledge of ritual (which is the ancient codified means whereby the attractive and expressive nature of the energies to be employed are organised and related), by his understanding of the "Words of Power" (which he discovers by experiment) and by using the potency of sound, the disciple of the future will work and build the new world with its culture and civilisation. A curious indication of the effect of the seventh ray magical work upon the mass consciousness is the growing use of slogans and of "catch phrases" (is that not the term used?) which are employed to bring about results and to sweep human beings into certain forms of mass action. This is the embryonic use of Words of Power, and from a study of their tonal values, their numerological indications and their inherent potency, men will eventually arrive at vast magical achievements and creations, producing group activity and the appearance of certain forms of expression upon the outer plane. After all, scientific formulas have reduced the most intricate and abstruse discoveries to a few signs and symbols. The next step is to embody these signs and symbols into a word or words, thus imparting to them what is esoterically called "the power of embodiment". If I might express it this way, the ancient statement that "God spoke and the worlds were made" simply means that God's formula for creation was reduced to a great Word which He sounded forth and the inevitable results followed. Something of this process on a tiny human scale will be seen happening in the coming age. At present, what I have said above may sound fanciful and fantastic to the average student.

It will be obvious to you that seventh ray disciples wield much power and for this reason the emphasis in all teaching given to them is laid upon *purity of motive*. In the past, the emphasis has been laid upon *purity of body* in the case of the sixth ray disciples. As was inevitable, they have carried the idea to a fanatical extent, and have stressed celibacy, asceticism and stringent rules of physical life, oft making sinful that which is natural. This has been a necessary stage in their development for it was essential that the physical plane should become a greater factor in their consciousness and that their attention should be turned from the realm of abstraction (which is their line of least resistance) and focussed upon physical living, for, again, energy follows thought. Thus their attitude to life could become more practical and the necessary integration take place. Disciples in the new age will lay the emphasis upon the mental principle, because it conditions thought and speech. All magical work is based upon the energy of thought and of the spoken word (the expression of the two magical centres referred to above) and purity in the realm of the mind and motive is regarded consequently as a basic essential.

The seventh ray influence is that which will produce in a peculiar and unexpected sense the Western School of Occultism just as the sixth ray impulse has produced the Eastern School of Occultism—the latter bringing the light down on to the astral plane and the new incoming influence carrying it down onto the physical. The Eastern teaching affected Christianity and indicated and determined the lines of its development and Christianity is definitely a bridging religion. The roles will eventually be reversed and the shift of the "light in the East" will be over Europe and America. This will inevitably bring about the needed and desired synthesis of the mystical way and the occult path. It will lead later to the formulation of the higher way; of this it is useless to speak at this time for you would not comprehend. None of the foundational and ancient *Rules of the Road* will ever be abrogated or discarded. Just as men used to travel on the ancient highways on foot, conforming to the requirement of their time and age, and today travel by rail or automobile (arriving at the same destination) so the same road will be followed, the same goal achieved but there may be different procedures, varying safeguards and changed protective measures. The rules may vary from time to time in order to provide easier indication and adequate protection. The training of the disciple in the future will differ in detail from that of the past but the basic rules remain authoritative.

The keynote, governing the development of the sixth ray disciple, was expressed for him in the words of Christ when He said: "I, if I be lifted up, will draw all men." The emphasis of all sixth ray work is Attraction and Repulsion—hence division and cleavage, producing eventually a realisation of the necessity for a consciously undertaken synthesis and integration, mentally motivated and produced. The history of Christianity (which is the history of Europe) will stand illumined if the Law of Attraction and Repulsion is studied in connection with its eventful past. The use and misuse of this law and its constant interpretations in terms of material desires, personal ambitions, and territorial control produced the many schisms and cleavages and will account for much that happened. Under the seventh ray influence, these cleavages will end and synthesis will eventually take place.

The keynote of the seventh ray disciple is "Radiatory Activity". Hence the emergence in world thought of certain new ideas—mental radiation or telepathy, the radiatory use of heat, the discovery of radium. All this connotes seventh ray activity.

The divine principle with which the seventh ray humanity will be mainly concerned is that of life as it expresses itself through the medium of the etheric body. It is for this reason that we find a growing interest in the nature of vitality; the function of the glands is being studied and before long their major function as vitality generators will be noted. Esoterically, they are regarded as externalisations upon the physical plane of the force centres in the etheric body and their aliveness or their lack of activity are indicative of the condition of those centres. The shift of the world interest is also into the realm of economics which is definitely the realm of life sustenance. Much is, therefore, bound to happen in all these spheres of interest, and once the etheric body becomes an established scientific fact and the centres—major and minor—are recognised as the foci of all energy as it expresses itself through the human body upon the physical plane, we shall see a great revolution take place in medicine, in diet and in the handling of daily life activity. This will produce great changes in the mode of work and labour and above everything else in the leisure activities of the race.

This thought brings to our attention the three methods of activity as employed by all the ray workers and which differ for each ray. Those which will eventually control the seventh ray types will gradually bring about changed attitudes to life and very different methods of daily living. These three are:

1. Group activity for the scientific relation of substance and energy.

Transformation from a Sixth to a Seventh Ray Cycle   61

2. The stimulation of etheric forms through rightly directed force.

3. The correct distribution, through scientific study, of vital energy.

We are entering a scientific age, but it will be a science which passes out of the impasse which it has now reached and which—having penetrated as it has into the realm of the intangible—will begin to work far more subjectively than heretofore. It will recognise the existence of senses which are super-sensory and which are extensions of the five physical senses, and this will be forced upon science because of the multitude of reliable people who will possess them and who can work and live in the worlds of the tangible and the intangible simultaneously. The mass of reputable testimony will prove incontrovertible. The moment that the subjective world of causes is proven to exist (and this will come through the indisputable evidence of man's extended senses) science will enter into a new era; its focus of attention will change; the possibilities of discovery will be immense and materialism (as that word is now understood) will vanish. Even the word "materialism" will become obsolete and men in the future will be amused at the limited vision of our modern world and wonder why we thought and felt as we did.

I would have you bear in mind in connection with the five rays which we have seen are influencing or beginning to influence humanity at this time (the first, second, third, sixth and seventh rays) that their effect varies according to the ray type or ray quality of the individual concerned and according to his position upon the ladder of evolution. Such points are often forgotten. If a man is, for instance, upon the second Ray of Love-Wisdom, it may be expected that the influence of that ray and of the sixth (which is along the second ray line of power) will be easily effective and will necessarily constitute the line of least resistance. This situation may, therefore, produce undue sensitivity and an unbalanced unfoldment of characteristics. It is our characteristics which influence our conduct and our reactions to circumstance. It will mean also that the influence of the first, third and seventh rays will be fundamentally unsettling and will call out resistance or—at the very least—an attitude of non-receptivity. In the world today, the rays which are along the line of energy which is that of the first Ray of Will or Power (including the third and the seventh) are in the ratio of three to two (as regards present manifestation) and, therefore, we can look for a fuller expression of the first ray attributes and happenings than would otherwise be the case. This will be particularly so because the sixth ray is fast going out of manifestation. All the above constitutes a piece of information which is of small value at this time. Its implications will become increasingly apparent as time goes on and I am, therefore, including them in my teaching.

DN 125-36

CHAPTER THREE

THE THREE DEPARTMENTS OF HIERARCHY

The Solar and Planetary Hierarchies

THE SOLAR HIERARCHY

The Solar Logos.

The Solar Trinity or Logoi

I	The Father	Will.
II	The Son	Love-Wisdom.
III	The Holy Spirit	Active Intelligence.

The Seven Rays
Three Rays of Aspect.
Four Rays of Attribute.

I. Will or Power...........II. Love-Wisdom............III. Active Intelligence.

4. Harmony or Beauty.
5. Concrete Knowledge.
6. Devotion or Idealism.
7. Ceremonial magic.

THE PLANETARY HIERARCHY
Sanat Kumara, the Lord of the World.
(The Ancient of Days.
The One Initiator.)

The Three Kumaras.
(The Buddhas of Activity.)
1   2   3

The reflections of the 3 major and 4 minor Rays.
The 3 Departmental Heads.

I. *The Will Aspect*	II. *The Love-Wisdom Aspect*	III. *Intelligence Aspect.*
A. The Manu.	B. The Bodhisattva. (The Christ. The World Teacher.)	C. The Mahachohan. (Lord of Civilisation)
b. Master Jupiter.	b. A European Master.	
c. Master M—.	c. Master K.H.	c. The Venetian Master.
	d. Master D.K.	4. The Master Serapis.
		5. Master Hilarion.
		6. Master Jesus.
		7. Master R—.

Four grades of initiates.

Various grades of disciples.

People on the Probationary Path.

Average humanity of all degrees.

CF 1239

The Work of the Mahachohan

Under the Manu work the regents of the different world divisions, such as, for instance, the Master Jupiter, the oldest of the Masters now working in physical bodies for humanity, Who is the regent for India, and the Master Rakoczi, Who is the regent for Europe and America. It must be remembered here that though the Master R., for instance, belongs to the seventh ray, and thus comes under the department of energy of the Mahachohan, yet in Hierarchical work He may and does hold office temporarily under the Manu. These regents hold in Their hands the reins of government for continents and nations, thus guiding, even if unknown, their destinies; They impress and inspire statesmen and rulers; They pour forth mental energy on governing groups, thus bringing about the desired results wherever co-operation and receptive intuition can be found amongst the thinkers.

IHS 46

As the seventh Ray of Organisation and of ceremonial work is now coming into prominence and manifestation, the work of the Master on that ray is that of synthesising, on the physical plane, all parts of the plan. The Master Rakoczi takes of the general plan as it is outlined in the inner Council Chamber and approximates it to the possible. He might be regarded as acting as the General Manager for the carrying out of the plans of the executive council of the Christ.

EXH 507-508

There is also a secret meaning here which relates to the seven rays as they express themselves in the human kingdom; the knowledge of this secret enables a Master to control epidemics and widespread diseases; with this you are not at this time concerned. Incidentally, the relative free-

The Three Departments of Hierarchy

dom from the plagues and epidemics which usually follow in the wake of war has been partly due to the use of this sevenfold knowledge by the Hierarchy, plus the scientific knowledge of humanity itself.

In this connection also (and I mention it simply from the angle of its interest) there are two hierarchical officials—the Mahachohan and His Representative upon the seventh ray—Who are today in possession of this secret in its entirety, and They are aided by five other Masters in applying the gained knowledge. These five Masters are working primarily with the deva evolution, and this is, as you know, connected with form, and in this particular case with the healing devas....

EH 598-599

The Master Who concerns Himself especially with the future development of racial affairs in Europe, and with the mental outgrowth in America and Australia, is the Master Rakoczi. He is a Hungarian, and has a home in the Carpathian mountains, and was at one time a well-known figure at the Hungarian Court. Reference to Him can be found in old historical books, and He was particularly before the public eye when he was the Comte de St. Germain, and earlier still when he was both Roger Bacon and later, Francis Bacon. It is interesting to note that as the Master R. takes hold, on the inner planes, of affairs in Europe, His name as Francis Bacon is coming before the public eye in the Bacon-Shakespeare controversy. He is rather a small, spare man, with pointed black beard, and smooth black hair, and does not take as many pupils as do the Masters previously mentioned. He is at present handling the majority of the third ray pupils in the occident in conjunction with the Master Hilarion. The Master R. is upon the seventh ray, that of Ceremonial Magic or Order, and He works largely through esoteric ritual and ceremonial, being vitally interested in the effects, hitherto unrecognised, of the ceremonial of the Freemasons, of the various fraternities, and of the Churches everywhere. He is called in the Lodge, usually, "the Count", and in America and Europe acts practically as the general manager for the carrying out of the plans of the executive council of the Lodge. Certain of the Masters form around the three great Lords an inner group, and meet in council with great frequency....

The Master P. works under the Master R. in North America. He it is Who has had much to do esoterically with the various mental sciences, such as Christian Science and New Thought, both of which are efforts put forth by the Lodge in an endeavour to teach men the reality of that which is not seen, and the power of the mind to create....

...This being the fifth sub-race of the fifth root-race, the pressure of the work on the five rays of mind which are controlled by the Mahachohan, is very great. The Masters are carrying an over heavy burden, and much of Their work of teaching disciples has been delegated to initiates and advanced disciples, and certain of the Masters on the first and second rays have temporarily taken over pupils in the Mahachohan's department.

IHS 58-61

...Two other Masters, specially concerned with the seventh or ceremonial ray, Whose particular work it is to supervise the development of certain activities within the next fifteen years, work under the Master R. Very definitely may the assurance be given here, that prior to the coming of the Christ, adjustments will be made so that at the head of all great organisations will be found either a Master, or an initiate who has taken the third initiation. At the head of certain of the great occult groups, of the Freemasons of the world, and of the various great divisions of the Church, and resident in many of the great nations will be found initiates or Masters. This work of the Masters is proceeding now, and all Their efforts are being bent towards bringing it to a successful consummation. Everywhere They are gathering in those who in any way show a tendency to respond to high vibration, seeking to force their vibration and to fit them so that they may be of use at the time of the coming of the Christ. Great is the day of opportunity, for when that time comes, through the stupendous strength of the vibration then brought to bear upon the sons of men, it will be possible for those who now do the necessary work to take a great step forward, and to pass through the portal of initiation.

IHS 61-62

On atmic levels, the levels of the spiritual will, are to be found the Ashrams of those Masters Who are interpreting the will of Shamballa and to Whom is committed the task of transmitting the purpose and organising the plans whereby that purpose can be fulfilled. As on manasic levels the Ashrams as a whole are presided over by the Master R., the Lord of Civilisation, so on buddhic levels all Ashrams are supervised by the Master K.H., with the aid of myself (the Master D.K.) and three senior and initiated disciples; the objective is the unfoldment of group awareness and of loving understanding, in order that the forms prepared and conditioned under the supervision of the Master R. may be sensitised and become increasingly conscious of reality through the development of an inner mechanism of light which—in its turn—will condition and develop the outer mechanism of contact....

RI 169-70

Let the fiat of the Lord go forth: The end of woe has come.

The ending of the present evil situation is, therefore, a cooperative measure; and here, in this connection, we have the appearance of the Lord of Civilisation Who voices and engineers upon the physical plane the fiat of the Lord of Liberation and of the Rider from the secret place. He aids and makes possible, owing to His control, the precipitating upon the Earth and in the arena of combat, of the power generated by the Lords of Liberation, expressed by the coming One and focussed through Him as the hierarchical Representative in Europe. The work of the Master R. has always been recognised as of a peculiar nature and as concerned with the problems of civilisation, just as the work of the Christ, the Master of all the Masters, is concerned with the spiritual development of humanity, and the work of the Manu is occupied with the science of divine government, with politics and law. Thus the incoming focussed energy, called forth in response to right invocation, is stepped down still nearer to humanity, and the masses can then respond to the new impulses. You have, therefore:

1. The Lords of Liberation, reached by the advanced spiritual thinkers of the world whose minds are rightly focussed.
2. The Rider on the white horse or from the secret place, reached by those whose hearts are rightly touched.
3. The Lord of Civilisation, the Master R., reached by all who, with the first two groups, can stand with "massed intent".

On the united work of these Three, if humanity can succeed in calling Them forth, will come the alignment and the correct relation of three great spiritual centres of the planet, a thing which has never occurred before. Then:

1. The Lords of Liberation will receive and transmit to the Hierarchy energy from the centre where *God's Will is known and furthered.*
2. The Rider will receive this energy and take such

action as will express it, plus the motivating energy from the centre *where God's Love is expressed.*

3. The Lord of Civilisation will stimulate and prepare the centre which we call humanity for right reception of this re-vitalising, stimulating and releasing force.

Thus Shamballa, the Hierarchy and Humanity will stand consciously related and dynamically in touch with each other. The Will of God, the Love of God and the Intelligence of God will thus fuse and blend on Earth and in relation to human problems. Conditions will consequently be brought about and energies will be set in motion which will end the rule of evil and bring war to an end through the victory of the Forces of Light, recognised and aided by Humanity.

EXH 274-75

...In 1932, the influence of the second ray began to assert itself and will continue to do so until 1945 when the seventh ray will swing slowly into activity. You will then have three rays producing simultaneous effects upon mankind:

1. The first Ray of Will or Power, expending its force.
2. The second Ray of Love-wisdom, reaching its meridian and holding the center of the stage until 1957.
3. The seventh Ray of Ceremonial Order, coming into activity in combination with the other two—the will-to-love and the will-to-order—producing beauty out of the present chaos.

The disciples, therefore, of the Master Morya, of the Master Koot Hoomi and of the Master Rakoczi are reaching out towards a period of the intensest activity. The destiny of the world lies in the hands of Their three groups of initiated disciples; with Them, the accepted disciples of the three groups are asked to cooperate and this offers opportunity to many everywhere. As they seek to vision the Plan, to cooperate with the three Masters and Their initiate groups, their opportunity will emerge. This triangle of energy is held responsible by the great Leaders in Shamballa for the regularising of world affairs. More than this it is not necessary for humanity to know.

DINAI 730

The energy which produces order. This is the energy of the seventh ray or power of divinity. At this time, its major expression will come through the relationships and adjustments required between capital and labour, and labour will be primarily involved. This energy is being assimilated in the Ashram of the Master...; at the inception of the industrial era He was responsible for the formation of the labour movement—a movement bringing into relation the workers of the world. It is interesting to have in mind that today labour functions internationally; it is a group which learns with rapidity and has in it the seeds of vast good; it is probably the group which will place goodwill in the forefront of human thinking—upon a pinnacle of thought. This Master to Whom I refer belongs to the Ashram of the Master R. He relieves Him of this phase of the work to be done.

EXH 646-47

We now come to a consideration of the vast Ashram controlled by the Master R. He is the Lord of Civilisation and His is the task of bringing in the new civilisation for which all men wait. It is a third ray Ashram, and therefore enfolds within its ring-pass-not all the Ashrams to be found upon the third Ray of Active Intelligence, upon the fifth Ray of Concrete Science and upon the seventh Ray of Ceremonial Order. All these Ashrams are working under the general direction of the Master R. He works primarily through the Masters of these three types of ray energy. He Himself at

The Three Departments of Hierarchy

this time is occupied with seventh ray energy, which is the order-producing energy upon our planet.

This is the Ray of Ceremonial Order, and through the activity of its energy, when correctly directed and used, a right rhythm is being imposed upon all aspects of human living. An effort is being constantly made to arrest the ugly chaos of the present and to produce the ordered beauty of the future. The major weapon now being used by the combined Forces of Evil is chaos, disruption, lack of established security, and consequent fear. The potency of these evil forces is exceedingly great because they belong to no one group of people and to all the ideologies. The chaos produced by indifference, the chaos produced by uncertainty, the chaos produced by fear, by starvation, by insecurity, by watching others suffer innocently, and the chaos produced by the warring and conflicting ambitious elements in every nation (*without exception*)—these are the factors with which the Master R. is attempting to deal; the task is one of supreme difficulty. The entire rhythm of international thinking has to be altered, and that constitutes a slow and arduous task; the evil personalities which, in every country, are responsible for the chaos and uncertainty, have eventually to be replaced by those who can work in cooperation with the rhythm of the seventh ray, and thus produce ordered beauty.

The task is further complicated by the fact that in the substitution of order for chaos, national cultures must be preserved and the outline of the new civilisation presented to the people. This major Ashram is therefore confronted with two elements in every land and nation: those people who hold on to the bad old things of the past, and those who work for the extreme opposite of this point of view and for that which is new. Under the influence of this seventh ray energy *balance has to be brought about* and preserved, so that the "noble middle way" of right action and of right human relations can be safely trodden. The task of the Master R. is, however, lightened by the fact that the seventh ray is now coming into activity and its potency is increasing year by year. His task is also aided by the intelligent work done by the Ashram of the English Master Who works consistently with the awakening and the arising masses.

Every October and every March, the Master R. gathers together His council of helpers, the Masters and the senior initiates in the Ashrams of the third, the fifth and the seventh rays. Though He is the Head of the third Ray of Aspect and is in control, therefore, of the two Rays of Attribute mentioned above, He does not Himself wield these forces, because He is One of the three Heads of the Hierarchy and His work cannot be confined to the activity of any one ray. He works through the Ashrams of these rays, but He Himself works primarily in cooperation with the Christ and the Manu.

EXH 667-69

...When...the Master R. assumed the task of Mahachohan or Lord of Civilisation, His Ashram was shifted from the seventh Ray of Ceremonial Order to the third Ray of Active Intelligence; the majority of those who have taken the second and the third initiations were transferred with Him under what might be called a "special dispensation"; the rest of the members of His Ashram remained for tuition and training in service under that Master Who took His place as the central point of the seventh ray Ashram.

DINAII 383

Hence the work of the Mahachohan at this time in connection with seventh ray (which is temporarily acting as the synthesis of the five types of energy over which He presides), might be summed up as follows:

First, He is utilising the seventh type of energy in order to further the recognition by the human unit of the subtler substance of the physical plane. This seventh ray is a primary factor in the production of objectivity. The energy of the planetary Logos of the seventh scheme dominates the seventh plane; it is the ray whereon deva substance and Spirit can meet and adapt themselves to each other with greater facility than on any other ray except the third.

Man, at present, is fully conscious, through some one or other of his senses, on the three lower subplanes; it is intended that he shall be equally conscious on the four higher. This has to be brought about by the stimulation of the deva substance which composes his bodies. This will be accomplished through the dynamic will of the transmitting devas as they energise the manipulatory devas, and thus affect the myriads of lesser lives which compose man's body, and also by an increased responsiveness of the indwelling man or thinker to the contact made upon his body. This increased awareness will be brought about by the arousing of the fifth spirilla, by the unfolding of the fifth petal in the egoic lotus, and by the gradual opening of the third eye through the arousing and uniform activity of five factors: the centre at the base of the spine, the three channels in the spinal column, and the pineal gland.

All these factors involve the activity of deva essence, plus the resultant awareness of the thinker. This will be followed by the conscious use of the newly-awakened powers. In this manner the close interrelation and interdependence of the two lines of evolution becomes magnificently apparent.

Second, the Mahachohan is working specifically at this time (in co-operation with the Manu), with the devas of the gaseous subplane; this is in connection with the destroying work they are to effect by the end of this rootrace, in order to liberate Spirit from constricting forms. Volcanic action therefore may be looked for, demonstrating in unexpected localities, as well as within the sphere of the present earthquake and volcanic zones. Serious disturbance may be looked for in California before the end of the century, and in Alaska likewise.

The work of the Mahachohan can also be seen in the effect that the devas of the kundalini fire are producing upon man. These are a peculiar group of Agnichaitans who have reached a stage of evolution which permits of their being separated off from their group into a group connected with a certain fire in man's bodies. This fire owing to its present activity, and the direction of that activity, is responsible for the reaction against physical marriage, and for the desire evinced by highly evolved men everywhere to evade the marriage relation, and confine themselves to creation upon the mental or astral planes. This is due to the present inclination of the manipulatory devas of the lower generative organs to seek the throat centre, and to function there, utilising the strength of the kundalini fire to bring this about. All this is under the law of evolution, but in the interim between cause and justified effect much harm, evasion of the law, and consequent suffering can be seen. Owing, therefore, to the violent reaction at this time against the safeguarding laws of civilisation, it has been decided that the nature and functions of the devas must be somewhat revealed to man, and that their place in the scheme of things, and man's close connection and dependence upon them, must be given out. At the same time, the means whereby they may be contacted, and the words whereby they can be controlled, will be withheld.

Laxness in the marriage relation, due to this particular cause, is only seen amongst the highly evolved and amongst the independent thinkers of the race. Similar laxness amongst the masses, and the low types of humanity, is

The Three Departments of Hierarchy

based upon a different reason, and their promiscuity is due to certain developments of the animal nature in its lowest manifestation. These two causes will bear consideration by those who have the present needs of civilisation at heart. They can then co-operate with the Mahachohan in the work of effecting the very necessary transfer of force from a lower to a higher centre, and prevent (through knowledge) the incidental license. This will bring about a refusal to besmirch the great love or sex impulse of nature.

The ceremonial ray has been often called "the marriage ritual of the Son", because upon this ray Spirit and matter can meet and have union. This fact also should be borne in mind during the next one hundred years, for they will see great changes in the marriage laws. The present laxity will inevitably bring a reaction, and the laws will become more stringent, in order to safeguard the race during a transition period. These laws will not be along the line of making escape from the marriage relation more difficult, but will take effect at the other end, so to speak; the rising generation will be properly taught and guarded, and indiscriminate, hasty marriage will not be permitted, nor will juveniles be allowed rashly to enter into the marriage obligation. There is no need to enlarge further upon this, for in working out their own problems men learn, and all that those upon the inner side are permitted to do is to give a hint or an indication.

Another angle of the Mahachohan's work at this time is connected with *sound,* and therefore with the particular devas whom we are considering. Through the mismanagement of men, and their unbalanced development, the sounds of earth, such as those of the great cities, of the manufactories, and of the implements of war, have brought about a very serious condition among the gaseous devas. This has to be offset in some way and the future efforts of civilisation will be directed towards the spreading of a revolt against the evils of congested living and to the dissemination of an impulse of a widespread nature to seek the country and wide spaces. One of the main interests in the future will be a tendency towards the elimination of noise, owing to the increased sensitiveness of the race. When the energy of water and of the atom is harnessed for the use of man, our present types of factories, our methods of navigation and of transportation, such as steamers and railway apparatus, will be entirely revolutionised. This will have a potent effect not only on man but on the devas.

CF 906-10

In connection with the Hierarchy, the central Triangle is composed of the Manu, representing loving intelligent *life*, the Christ, representing loving intelligent *consciousness*, and the Mahachohan, representing loving intelligent *activity*, and therefore between Them representing every phase of group livingness, group expression and group action; these qualities focus through the Mahachohan, primarily because He is the Lord of Civilization and the civilizations of humanity represent progressive growth and unfoldment.

TEL 185

The Seventh Ray Ashram

The seven major Ashrams are each responsive to one of seven types of ray energy and are focal points in the Hierarchy of the seven rays. The central, senior and major Ashram is (at this time) the repository of second ray energy, as this ray governs this second solar system. It is the Ashram of Love-Wisdom—the Ashram in which the Buddha and the Christ received Their initiations and through which each of Them works. It will be obvious that if the process of invocation and evocation governs the interplay of the planetary centres, you have in this fact another reason why the senior Ashram is second ray in quality. Invocation is related to radiation. Evocation is related to magnetism. These are two points worthy of your consideration.

The other six major Ashrams came sequentially into being as the invocation of primitive man reached such a point of intensity of expression that a response was evoked from Shamballa, via its ray Representatives, working with directed energy in the three worlds. A "point of radiatory force" was established, at first in relation to the second ray Ashram, and later to the other Ashrams. One by one, as the rays cycled into activity in the three worlds and eventually on the physical plane, the seven Ashrams were founded, developed and expanded until the time arrived—several aeons ago—when all seven Ashrams were fully organised, and through them passed a steady flow of human beings liberating themselves from the three worlds.

In the earliest times this flow of disciples was exceedingly small. One by one, individual aspirants found their way out of the ranks of humanity and inside the ring-pass-not of the Hierarchy. In the beginning, only the first two initiations were given and only through the instrumentality of the second ray; and at these initiations the World Teacher of the period officiated.

Then at a time when the seventh Ray of Ceremonial Order (the ray which plays so potent and mysterious a part in the phase of discipleship called initiation) was in cyclic activity, a much greater number of disciples appeared, prepared for initiation; the initiatory process was then administered in a seventh ray Ashram; this seventh ray Ashram was the second to be formed, owing to the fact that the seventh ray is the relating factor between life and matter upon the form side. Again, so the ancient Archives tell us, there came a great crisis in the evolution of humanity; this necessitated one of the rare cyclic changes which have distinguished the fluid policy of the Hierarchy. Men began to demonstrate responsiveness to the Law of Integration and *personality* appeared with all its potentiality for good and evil. Man became an integrated unit in the three worlds. A great possibility then emerged; man could, through training and the use of the mind, make contact with the soul. This had not hitherto been done except to a slight degree. This crisis therefore led to the creation, or rather to the appearance, of the initiatory process to which we have given the name of the third initiation....

Since that time [when the Christ took the fifth and sixth initiations—*Editors*], all the seven major Ashrams have been fully organised and are steadily increasing in radiatory activity. As you will have noted, the order of their appearance—under ray activity—was 2, 7, 4, 6, 5, 3, 1. In giving this item of ashramic information I am giving you more hints than you will immediately realise.

RI 383-87

...Four factors lie behind the momentous happening of the release of this form of atomic energy, through the medium of what is erroneously and unscientifically called the "splitting of the atom". There are other factors, but you may find the following four of real interest:....

A concerted effort was made by a number of disciples who were working in fifth and seventh ray ashrams, and this enabled them to impress lesser disciples in the scientific field and helped them to surmount the well-nigh insuperable difficulties with which they were confronted.

EXH 495

Under the influence of disciples on the seventh Ray of Organisation or of Ceremonial Order, that powerful physical concretisation of energy which we call "money" is proving a topic of the most definite concentration; it is being most carefully considered, and the minds of thinking financiers and of wealthy humanitarian persons and philanthropists will be gradually led forward from a strictly philanthropic activity to an activity which is impulsed and brought into expression by spiritual insight, and by *a recognition of the claims of Christ* (no matter by what name He may be called in the East or in the West) upon the financial reservoir of the world. This is a hard thing to bring about, for the subtle energies of the inner worlds take much time in producing their effects upon the objective, tangible plane of divine manifestation. Money is not yet used divinely, but it will be. Nevertheless, the task is well in hand and is engaging the attention of disciples upon all the rays, under the guidance and the impression of the powerful seventh ray Ashram—now already in process of externalisation.

DINAII 221-22

The study of this *Science of Applied Purification* is one which is engrossing the attention of all the ashrams at this time; disciples in the first ray ashram, in the second ray ashram, and in the seventh ray ashram are peculiarly active along these lines, for the destruction of evil is the work of the first ray, and in so destroying its effects purity is achieved; the fostering of good then becomes possible and is the work of the second ray, of the Builders; and the bringing of spiritual energy into contact with substance, and consequently with matter, is the unique work of the seventh ray because it is now in manifestation. The rays which are active and in manifestation at this time and in this cycle are there in conformity to the Plan and in preparation for the externalisation of the Hierarchy and the reappearance of the Christ. These rays are particularly involved, and therefore the initiates and the disciples in the ashrams of the Masters are also particularly implicated.

EXH 693

In London, in New York, in Geneva and Darjeeling and in Tokyo, a Master will eventually be found, organising a major energy centre; at the same time His Ashram will continue to function upon buddhic levels, for the entire personnel has not been alerted for externalisation. The Ashram will therefore be working on two levels—and yet that is not a correct statement of fact, as there are no levels, as well you know, but only states of consciousness. Ask me not how this can be; ponder on the relation of this dual and simultaneous appearance by attempting to grasp the nature of the manifested form of the planetary Logos in the Person of Sanat Kumara. Sanat Kumara is not the personality of the planetary Logos, for personality as you understand it is not existent in His case. It is not the soul of the planetary Logos, because that soul is the anima mundi and the soul of all forms in all kingdoms. Sanat Kumara, the Eternal Youth, can be seen by Those Who have the right, presiding, for instance, over the Council in Shamballa, yet at the same time He is present as the life and the informing intelligence upon and within our planet.

You have therefore five points where the externalisation of the Ashrams will take place and eventually be focussed. From these points, as time elapses, other Ashrams, subsidiary in nature, will be found emerging, sponsored and founded by disciples and initiates from these five Ashrams, and representing the three major rays and two minor rays. To start with, they will be founded through the presence in these localities of some senior or world disciple; it must be remembered that the forerunner of all movements which appear upon the physical plane is an educational propaganda, therefore some disciple upon the second ray will come into action, first of all, in all these five points; he will be followed by a disciple upon the seventh ray. All world movements are, as well you know, externalisations of subjective ideas and concepts and of phases of formulated thinking; and the appearance of the Hierarchy upon earth in tangible form is no exception to this rule.

EXH 676-77

CHAPTER FOUR

ASTROLOGY AND THE SEVENTH RAY

These interlocking energies which play through, traverse, return, stimulate and energise every part of our solar system...only evoke conscious response where the vehicle of expression and of response is adequate to the impact, and this statement is true of the solar Logos, the planetary Logoi, and of all forms in all the kingdoms upon our planet. Unconscious reaction will of course exist, but it will be on a general or mass scale, and much of it pours through to us from these distant constellations, via the fifth Creative Hierarchy. This Hierarchy, being on the verge of liberation, is to be found on the intellectual level of consciousness and can, therefore, be used as a focal point and a transmitter of the higher energies to our solar system and to the planet. If you make a careful study of the chart of the twelve Creative Hierarchies...you will note that this Hierarchy is influencing, and is influenced by, the seventh Ray of Magical Order and of Ceremonial Organisation. The basic function of this ray is to relate spirit and matter and produce the manifested form. The sign of the zodiac with which it is closely connected is that of Cancer, the Crab, which is a mass sign and one of the "gates" into manifested life.

EA 32-33

Earlier in this treatise, I gave you the relation between the rays and the constellations and stated that each of the seven rays expressed itself through the medium of three constellations or through a triangle of energies. This relation is the basis of the entire Science of Triangles and, therefore, of astrology itself; it is also related to the rays, the constellations, their ruling planets and our Earth in a great synthesis of energies; it relates our solar system to the larger whole and our tiny non-sacred planet to the solar system. Let me repeat that statement and thus indicate to you some vital facts anent this world of interweaving energies. The Rays pour through, are expressed by and are transmitted through the following constellations:

```
Ray I ................. Aries ................. Leo ................. Capricorn
Ray II................. Gemini ............ Virgo .............. Pisces
Ray III .............. Cancer ............ Libra .............. Capricorn
Ray IV .............. Taurus.............. Scorpio .......... Sagittarius
Ray V................. Leo ................... Sagittarius ...... Aquarius
Ray VI .............. Virgo ................ Sagittarius ...... Pisces
Ray VII ............ Aries ................. Cancer............ Capricorn
```

EA 489

Uranus is the exoteric ruler of Aquarius; it is also the esoteric ruler of Libra and the hierarchical ruler of Aries. It is peculiarly active at this time and brings in the energy of the seventh ray. The circulating of its energies can be portrayed by the following symbol or diagram:

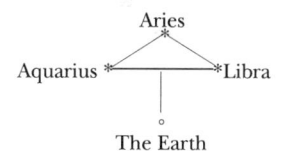

```
                Aries
                  *
    Aquarius *─────────*Libra
                  │
                  ○
              The Earth
```

This triple inflow of seventh ray energy, coloured by the force of three great constellations, is potent to effect major changes in our little planet. It is interesting to realise that Aries, the Inaugurator, is rendered effective on the Earth through the organising potency of Uranus. Aries is the source, the beginning and the initiator of the New Age and its coming civilisations, of the appearance of the kingdom of God on earth and also of the individual initiate into the Mysteries. Aquarius is the present Determiner of the future. That which is now initiated in Aries will become manifested in Aquarius, and Libra will enforce the achievement of a point of balance or (esoterically speaking) of the "escape from opposing forces at the midway point between the source and the goal".

EA 548

It is only in the present cycle that the Sun and Moon "veil" certain planets and are the exoteric symbols for certain esoteric forces. As evolution proceeds, the planets will not be veiled. Their influences will not be so remote. At present the mechanism of the majority of the human family is not tuned to the reception of the rays from Vulcan, Uranus or Neptune whilst Pluto at present only evokes response from groups or from those disciples who are enough evolved rightly to respond. The three veiled planets—Vulcan, Uranus, and Neptune—are all sacred planets, embodying first, seventh and sixth ray energies. Vulcan is never an exoteric ruler and only comes into real activity when a man is on the Path, whilst Uranus and Neptune are rulers of the eleventh and twelfth houses, and govern Aquarius and Pisces. The implications will be clear to you.

EA 509

Aries

Uranus embodies the energy of the seventh ray and its work is analogous to that of Mercury, for the seventh ray is the ray which relates spirit and matter and brings together electric fire and fire by friction, thus producing manifestation. Uranus leads the soul to the burning ground during the final stages of the Path, when the fire of Aries and the fires engendered through the potency of Uranus produce the flaming heat of the final burning ground. Through this burning ground, the initiate has finally to pass. Uranus rules the occult Way and is, in an esoteric sense, connected with the Hierophant of the Mysteries of

Initiation.

Therefore, we have in relation to Aries and the life of the soul, which there comes into subjective manifestation, certain related signs wherein the soul, in objective manifestation, passes through peculiar and definite crises:

1. The crises of the battlefield, leading to the culminating battle in Scorpio and the liberation into life in Capricorn, the place of the higher initiations, after the reversal of the wheel.
2. The crisis of the birth place in Virgo, brought about through the activity of Mercury, leading through Leo to the birth of the Christ in Capricorn. The self-conscious individual in Leo becomes the Christ-conscious Initiate in Capricorn.
3. The crisis of the burning ground, which is brought about through the activity of Uranus. This is entered through the free choice of the initiate who makes his choice in Libra, the point of balance where—usually—the moment for the reversal of the wheel takes place. There the man has to decide whether to proceed as usual and according to custom or, reversing the wheel, to pass through the burning ground to liberation. Libra is the polar opposite to Aries and therefore closely related.

You will note that the rays which are related to or expressing themselves through Aries are curiously balanced, rays 1 and 7 are the highest and the lowest, and therefore demand a point of balance upon the wheel which is provided in Libra. Rays 6 and 4 bring to this balancing process the energy of the second ray, the major building ray which enables the man to build anew and provide himself with a spiritual body of manifestation.

EA 100-1

Gemini

...Only one ray is, therefore, lacking where Gemini is concerned, and that is the seventh Ray of Organisation, Ceremonial Magic and Ritual. This accounts for the instability and the fluidity of the Gemini influence, and is largely responsible for the frequent failure of the Gemini person to express the beauty, ideals, etc., which are sensed so that they materialise upon the physical plane. The seventh ray produces fixation upon the exoteric level of experience and "anchors" (if I may use such a term) the ray forces into form, producing concrete expression of the subjective realities or powers. Six forces meet in Gemini and, for this reason, the double triangle or King Solomon's seal is one of the subjective symbols of this sign, linking it again with the Masonic tradition and indicating also again the essential dualism of this sign.

All the inner potencies are, therefore, present and only the stabilising seventh ray energy is omitted from the dowry of the man born in Gemini. Thus we can easily account for the versatility of the Gemini subject. The effectiveness of Mercury is also enhanced in its interpretive aspect because the Gemini person can always find points of contact with people on nearly every ray. This is an interesting point to remember if you will realise that the great Masonic ritual was inaugurated under the influence of this sign, and yet—the ray of ritual was omitted. This is due to the fact of reaction, producing opposition and therefore interplay and struggle. Hence the tests and trials of the Masonic procedure.

EA 364

RAYS

City	Soul	Personality	Sign
1. London	5th	7th	Gemini

EA 458

Cancer

Scorpio is also most interestingly connected with the constellation, Cancer, through the influences of the sixth ray, for it should be remembered that that ray is also expressing itself through Neptune, but in a spiritual and esoteric manner. Neptune governs Cancer esoterically. The significance is therefore clear, for Cancer is the sign of birth; it is the door into incarnation and the sign of generation. Scorpio is the sign of sex and of regeneration, and birth is ever the intended result of the sex relation. Father-spirit and Mother-matter when brought together produce the Son. The tests and difficulties and pains of this era are symptoms or indications of the "entering into manifestation" of the new civilisation and culture. They portend the birth of the new era for which the entire world waits. This will happen if—speaking esoterically—the sixth ray energy of Mars is transmuted into the sixth ray energy of Neptune, for the one is "objective and full of blood" and the other is "subjective and full of life".

A great mystery is veiled and hidden in the above relationship, for Cancer-Neptune is expressive of the seventh ray which rules and controls the eighth Creative Hierarchy. This is one of the five Hierarchies whose names are unknown to us and this particular one stands upon the verge of liberation. At the same time it is closely connected with the mind principle as it works out through the solar Angels or through the human hierarchy. It is related to the birth of the fourth Creative Hierarchy in a sense not to be understood by anyone below the stage of the fourth initiation, but it is an interesting fact to remember for it is in the connection between the sixth and seventh rays that that potent "desire for incarnation" was aroused which resulted in the fall of the angels in primordial times....

EA 217-8

Leo

It will be apparent to you (given a little thought) that the Sun, as it veils Neptune, produces a potent effect upon the personality, symbolised for us here by the astral body, whilst Uranus (which is also veiled by the Sun) symbolises the effect of the soul upon the personality. Hence the activity of the seventh ray, which is—from one angle—the lowest aspect of the first ray. Hence you have also the underlying idea of:

1. The awakening of the personality to soul control and contact, with a true expression eventually, in the three worlds, of soul-will, desire and intent.

2. The awakening of the seventh centre, the centre at the base of the spine, by the soul working through the first or highest head centre and producing (as a consequence) the surging upwards of the kundalini fire. This, in its turn, produces fusion with the higher forces. When this takes place the three major centres in the body are

The Head	*The Heart*	*The Base of Spine*
Central spiritual Sun	The heart of the Sun	The physical Sun.
Sirius	Mercury	Saturn
The Sun	Uranus	Neptune

As the above alignment corresponds to a very high stage of initiation, it will not be possible to grasp all the implications, but enough may be apparent to reveal the underlying theme and purpose of the great work....

I would here call to your attention that, through these directing planets, the following rays are controlling factors in the chart of the Leo subject:

1. The Sun—2nd ray—love-wisdom.
2. Uranus—7th ray—organisation or directed manifestation.
3. Neptune—6th ray—idealistic one-pointedness. Devotion to an objective.

In the perfected Leo, the loving self-conscious soul (2nd ray) carries its power of expression straight through from its own plane to the plane of exterior manifestation, but preserves at the same time its interior control (Uranus) and from that point of achievement, proceeds to make its ideal objective (Neptune) a fact in consciousness, through sensitivity to the higher vibration and directed intelligent service of the Plan. Ponder on this summation.

When Uranus controls, the Leo person is significantly the true observer, detached from the material side of life, but utilising it as he pleases. His spiritual consciousness is capable of great expression and he can be (as has oft been pointed out by astrologers) both an electric, dynamic leader, a pioneer in new fields of endeavour and also a magnetic centre of a group whether the group is small, as in a home, or vast as in a nation....

EA 300-309

Libra

Uranus is the esoteric ruler and is of supreme importance in this sign for the seventh ray works through this planet and is the embodiment of the principle of concretion and the materialising of that which is in need of objective manifestation, through the bringing together of spirit and matter. It is here that the whole mystery of money lies hid and the creation and production of money. I would like here to point out to you that it is with the third aspect of divinity and the third aspect alone that the creative process is concerned. It is through the relation of the three aspects of the third divine manifestation—law, affinity and concretised energy—that money is created.

EA 246

Scorpio

The place of the planets in this sign is also most revealing, and in line also with the general purpose of the experience in Scorpio....Uranus is exalted in Scorpio; the power of Venus is lessened in this sign, whilst the Moon falls. What do these facts symbolically portray? Let me see if I can make the beauty of these implications clear to you.

Uranus is the planet whose characteristics are the scientific mind, which, at this stage of the disciple's career, means that he can begin to live the occult life and the way of divine knowledge can take the place of the mystic way of feeling. It means also that knowledge can be transmuted into the way of wisdom and of light. This necessarily brings in the will aspect or the influence of the first ray (Vulcan) blended with the seventh ray (Uranus) producing the desired manifestation upon the physical plane. Uranus, therefore, initiates a new order of life and conditions and this—when developed in the life of the disciple—in its turn produces an understanding of the causes of things as they are, and the desire to change the old order and the old orientation into the new. This produces the reversal of the wheel. This can be seen happening today most clearly in connection with humanity and with world processes. Carried forward to its logical conclusion, the influence of Uranus finally produces an unfolded spiritual consciousness in contradistinction to the human; for this reason, Uranus is exalted in this sign and assumes a position of power and of directed influence.

EA 224-25

Aquarius

The rulers of Aquarius are of a peculiar interest. They constitute an effective group of planets and bring in the influences of the seventh, second and fourth rays. These are pre-eminently the rays which determine the final stages of man's progress as well as the initial stages, being more potent at the beginning of the involutionary path and the end of the evolutionary path than they are in the middle period. They determine the final stages and happenings of the Path of Initiation. The seventh ray brings into expression upon the physical plane the major pairs of opposites—spirit and matter—and relates them to each other, producing eventually one functioning whole. The second ray gives soul expression and spiritual consciousness and also the power to pour out love and wisdom upon earth whilst the fourth ray indicates the field of service and the mode of attaining the goal. This mode or method is that of conflict and struggle in order to reach harmony and thus express all truly human characteristics, for the fourth ray and the fourth Creative Hierarchy constitute essentially one expression of truth.

Some astrologers assign Saturn as one of the rulers. Alan Leo does so, but I would point out that in this case he is dealing entirely with the progress of the ordinary man upon the wheel of life, and the Saturn which he senses as ruling Aquarius is the Saturnian influence of Capricorn, in which sign Saturn governs in two fields. On the reversed wheel, the Saturnian influence exhausts itself in Capricorn and the man is then free from karma and needs no presentation of opportunity for he stands a free initiate, a true Master Mason and can then proceed with world service undeterred and held back by no thought of self or selfish desire. He comes then under the influence of Uranus, that mysterious and occult planet. His will is focussed and developed by the Uranian influences and he develops into a leader. He brings about desired changes and produces those new conditions which will help the soul of humanity to express itself more freely. Water being the symbol of substance and of material expression plus emotional motivation, Aquarius is consequently dual in its activity, and the third ray expresses itself powerfully through this sign, reaching our planet through Uranus and the Moon which hides or veils Uranus symbolically in this case. There is, therefore, to be found the double influence of Uranus, expressing the quality and bringing in the energies of the seventh ray, in one case, and the third ray in the other. The seventh ray is, in the last analysis, the focussed differentiated energy of ray one as it expresses the will of the first aspect of divinity on earth through the power to relate and bring into objective manifestation—by an act of the will—both spirit and matter. This it brings about through the activity of ray three, expressing itself through humanity and its individual units, though combining with the energy of the three rays which are released through the ruling planets:

1. Uranus—ray seven—The will to be and to know simultaneously on all planes of manifestation.
2. Jupiter—ray two—The fusion of heart and mind, which is the subjective purpose of manifestation. This is brought about through the third and seventh ray activity on the exoteric wheel.
3. The Moon—ray four—The will to be and to know plus the fusion of heart and mind is the result of the work carried forward in the fourth Creative Hierarchy under the influence of that energy which produces harmony through conflict.

EA 137-39

Aquarius relates humanity to the Pleiades and therefore to Taurus in an unusual manner. The key to this relation is to be found in the word desire, leading, through the transmutative processes of life experience, to aspiration and finally the relinquishing of desire in Scorpio. Aquarius, Alcyone and Humanity constitute a most interesting triangle of force. Alcyone is one of the seven Pleiades and is called the "star of the Individual" and sometimes the "star of intelligence". It was potently active during the previous solar system wherein the Third Person of the Trinity was peculiarly omnipotent and active, just as today the cosmic Christ, the Second Person of the Trinity, is peculiarly active in this solar system. The energies coming from Alcyone impregnated the substance of the universe with the quality of mind. As a consequence of this most ancient activity, the same force was present at the time of individualisation in this solar system, for it is in this system, and primarily upon our planet, the Earth, that the major results of that early activity have made themselves felt. Two of our planets, the Earth (non-sacred) and Uranus (sacred), are directly the product of this third ray activity. This is of great importance to remember. I would also ask you to link this thought with the teaching that through the divine centre of intelligent activity which we call humanity, the fourth kingdom in nature will eventually act as the mediating principle to all the three lower kingdoms. Humanity is the divine Messenger to the world of form; it is essentially Mercury, bringing light and life to other divine manifestations and of this all divine world Saviours are the eternal symbols.

This coming process of planetary service through the third divine centre is only truly effective when Aquarius rules and when our sun is passing through that sign of the zodiac. Hence the immense importance of the next 2000 years. Therefore, only when a man is a world server and becoming group conscious can this desired objective of manifestation begin to demonstrate. It is beginning to happen today for the first time in planetary history. It is one of the first fruits of initiation and only in the next root race to our present Aryan race will we begin really to understand the significance of the process and the true nature of the energies to be released through the medium of humanity upon the planet. It is for this reason that Jupiter and Uranus (expressions of the second and the seventh rays) are the exoteric and esoteric rulers of Aquarius.

You have, therefore, the following line of force to study:

1. Alcyone—in the Pleiades, the mothers of the seven aspects of form life and the "wives of the seven Rishis of the Great Bear". They are connected with the Mother aspect which nurtures the infant Christ.
2. Aquarius—the World Server, the transmitter of energy which evokes magnetic response.
3. Jupiter and Uranus—planets of beneficent consummation. The second ray of love and the seventh ray which fuses spirit and matter "to the ultimate glory" of the solar Logos are in the fullest eventual cooperation.
4. Humanity — the focal point for all these energies and the divine distributor of them to individual man and later to the lower three kingdoms in nature.

EA 200-01

Leo, Capricorn and Pisces

The effects produced are mass effects and the Rulers of these constellations which move into activity at this time are those listed in one of the earlier tabulations which I gave you.

Leo.—Ruler: The Sun, veiling Uranus, the planet of occultism, and that which governs group relations, organisations and the eleventh House. It relates the Leo influence to Aquarius.

Capricorn.—Ruler: Venus, governing the second House, which is concerned with economics, the distribution of money and metals and which rules Taurus, the "seed house" of illumination and the new emerging light. Venus also rules Libra exoterically and the seventh House wherein enemies are recognised and unions and friendships achieved.

Pisces.—Ruler: Pluto, governing the eighth House, the

house of death, of dissolution, of detachment and ruling Scorpio, the sign of testing and of discipleship.

This tabulation and its inferred relationships warrant careful study in the light of modern affairs and the present world situation. From the angle of the ray energies involved and seeking to control human life, you have the influence of the seventh Ray of Ceremonial Law, Order and Magic, the fifth Ray of Concrete Knowledge, or Science and the first Ray of Will unitedly bringing about fundamental changes, and ushering in the new era. This combination is terrifically potent and brings about the precipitation of inner forces, an increased activity of the lower mind and an out-pouring of the Shamballa force—all three of which can be seen functioning in the field of the planetary life today as never before. The greater effect is produced owing to the greatly increased sensitivity of mankind, compared to the two other times in which (in cyclic evolution) these three constellations were active. The combination is seen demonstrating in human affairs today. It was responsible for the organisation which lay behind the World War—an organisation involving all three levels in the threefold world of human evolution and which affects also the three kingdoms in nature, climaxing in the fourth. It is responsible for the use of mental power on a vast scale, notably in the material sense as at present and for the achievement of human desire, plus the self-will of an evil few, who, because of the seeds of evil in their own nature, respond to the lower aspects of this force. It is also responsible for the steadily mounting will-to-good of the awakening many.

A close analysis of these constellations, their planetary rulers and the ray forces which these transmit will clarify the world issues in an amazing manner, plus an appreciation of the houses in which these effects will primarily be felt. The following brief tabulation may prove useful, even if it is only a repetition of that earlier said:

Constellation	Ruler	Ray	House
Leo	The Sun (Uranus)	Seventh	Eleventh
Capricorn	Venus	Fifth	Second and Seventh
Pisces	Pluto	First	Eighth

The energies poured out therefore, will be felt primarily in those aspects of human living which are influenced by the rulers of certain houses.

The seventh Ray of Ceremonial Order or Organisation is felt in the house of relationships, of organisations and of mutual effort and of aspiration (either towards good or evil). The forces of this ray work out on the seventh or physical plane—the plane whereon major changes in all forms are made and on which the disciple must firmly stand as he takes initiation.

This seventh ray sweeps into organised and directed activity the world of forces upon the outer sphere of manifestation, and produces the precipitation of Karma, which, in this case leads to:

1. The working out into expression of all the subjective evil of the life of humanity, thus producing the world war.

2. The initiation of the planetary Logos and—with Him—of all who take their stand upon the side of the Forces of Light. This takes various forms as far as humanity is concerned:

    a. The initiation of the consciousness of the masses of men into the Aquarian Age, bringing them under the new influences and potencies, and enabling them to make a response of which they would not otherwise be capable.

    b. The initiation of the aspirants of the world on to the Path of Accepted Discipleship.

c. The bringing about of certain major initiations in the case of those world disciples who are ready enough and strong enough to take them.

In spite of the vast destruction everywhere, the work of the seventh ray is being increasingly felt; the destruction of the forces of evil is going on even though at great cost to the Forces of Light; simultaneously there is a regrouping and a rearrangement of human attitudes and thought; this is brought about as a result of the tremendous demand upon the world thinkers for direction and guidance. Thus the nebulous structure and the dim outlines of the New Age civilisation can already be seen.

The underlying spirit of freedom will triumph as it is organised into revolt against slavery. To this end, the seventh ray will increasingly make contribution.

EA 538-41

At the same time, it will be obvious to you that, in relation to these simple triangles, certain interlocking triangles also emerge, as for instance the zodiacal triangle of *Leo–Pisces–Capricorn* and the allied planetary triangle of *Saturn–Uranus–Mercury*. These two triangles pour their six streams of force into our three planetary centres at this time, vitalising and stimulating the planetary triangle of *Shamballa–Hierarchy–Humanity*. Behind these three stands a cosmic triangle, emanating three streams of energy which pour into and through the three lesser triangles, thus potently affecting every kingdom in nature. This cosmic triangle is that of the *Great Bear–Sirius–the Pleiades*. This paragraph simply summarises the preceding pages and indicates the relation between the four triangles of energy...

It is interesting to note that the seventh Ray of Ceremonial Law and Order works through Uranus which is today the transmitter of Sirian force via Pisces to the Hierarchy. From that "middle centre" it passes to that sensitive band of disciples, aspirants and workers to whose hearts and hands is committed the heavy task, incident to the re-organisation and the rebuilding of the shattered world structure. The seventh ray has sometimes been called a peculiar name by Knowers. It is regarded as the "Ray of Ritualistic Decency". It aids and inaugurates the appearing of a new world order, based on a spiritual drive and on aspiration, mental freedom, loving understanding and a physical plane rhythm which provides opportunity for full creative expression. To bring this about, energy from Shamballa (embodying the will-to-good) is fused and blended with the organising energy of the seventh ray and then carried to humanity along the stream of love which emanates from the Hierarchy itself. Pisces governs this effort of the Hierarchy because the highest aspect of Pisces which humanity can at this time in any way comprehend is that of Mediatorship. This is the energy of mediation, of right relationship. Today as never before the Hierarchy stands as a "mediating transmitter" between:

1. Humanity and the will of God. The revelation of the true significance and purpose of that will as it stands behind all world events is needed now as never before. This can come through a closer relation between the Hierarchy and Humanity.
2. Humanity and its karma, for it is equally essential that the laws for the transmutation of karma into active present good are clearly grasped.
3. Humanity and cosmic evil, focussed for many millennia of years in what has been called the Black Lodge. Speculation anent this Lodge and its activities is both fruitless and dangerous.

The latter fact is responsible for the widespread attack

made upon Masonry during this century. Masonry—inadequate and corrupt as it has been and guilty of overemphasising certain forms of symbols—is nevertheless a germ or seed of future hierarchical effort when that effort is—at some later date—externalised on Earth. Masonry is governed by the seventh ray, and when certain important changes have been made and the spirit of Masonry is grasped instead of the letter, then we shall see a new form of hierarchical endeavour appear to aid in the restoration of the ancient and sacred Mysteries among men.

The energy of Uranus, pouring upon and into humanity, produces the urge to better conditions to provide better forms for the occult and esoteric life and to blend more adequately the inner and the outer man. This is one of the reasons why the Moon is spoken of so often as veiling Uranus. The Moon is frequently used as a blind when Uranus is meant. Today the Moon is a dead world and the reason is that the Uranian urge became so strong in that far distant time when there were living forms upon the Moon that it led to the complete and final evacuation of the Moon and the transfer of its life to our planet. Such a transfer is not necessary today as the consciousness of humanity is such that the needed changes can be brought about without such a drastic procedure. It is, however, this Uranian influence which lies behind the present shift of populations throughout Europe and Great Britain and which is responsible for the steady movement of peoples from East to West, from Asia to Europe in the earlier history of that continent and from Europe to the Western hemisphere in more modern times.

In the study of the interlocking of these triangles, it will become apparent to the student that the combination of the influences of Sirius, Leo and Uranus has been much needed at this time to foster and bring about those conditions which will enable mankind, under the steady influence of the Hierarchy, to take the first initiation and "give birth to the Christ", thus revealing and bringing to the light of day the inner, hidden, spiritual Man. It is in Leo that man undergoes the preparatory stages of this first initiation. He finds himself and becomes self-conscious; then he arrives at the stage of intelligent discipleship; he formulates a conscious inner programme or purpose under the steady pressure of the life of the indwelling Christ; he begins to exhaust and deny the demands and desires of the lower nature. This cycle of experience is followed by a painful life of conscious re-orientation—a cycle wherein he achieves balance and begins to "stand in spiritual Being" as a result of constant trial and testing. Finally he stands ready for *the ordeal and accolade of fire, preceding the first initiation.* At that final stage, Humanity today stands. When (as is now the case) the influence of Uranus is added to the other influences and the seventh ray is at the same time entering into a major cycle of activity on the Earth, there is then present the energy needed to precipitate the crisis of initiation and produce a great rhythmic awakening. Astrologers would find it of interest to note similar combinations in the individual horoscope.

EA 441-47

CHAPTER FIVE

THE PSYCHOLOGY OF NATIONS

Seventh Ray Nations

All of the great nations are controlled by two rays, just as is the human being. With the smaller nations we need not concern ourselves. All the nations are controlled by a personality ray, which is the dominant potent and main controlling factor at this time, and by a soul ray which is sensed only by the disciples and the aspirants of any nation.

This soul ray must be evoked into an increased functioning activity by the New Group of World Servers, for this is one of their main objectives and tasks. This must never be lost to sight. Much could be written about the historical influence of the rays during the past two thousand years and of the way in which great events have been influenced or brought about by the periodic ray influence. Interesting as it is and indicative of the present national trends and problems, all that I can now do is to point out the energies governing each nation, and leave you to study and note their effect and to comprehend their relation to the present condition of the world. One thing I would point out and that is that those rays which govern a particular nation and which are at this time actively working are very potent, either materially or egoically; some of the problems may be due to the fact that certain rays, governing certain nations, are not at this time active.

DN 49

Russia

A careful analysis of the idealism of Russia and of the United States may reveal no resemblances in the goal of their idealism; the Russian is driven by his seventh ray soul towards the imposition of an enforced ceremonial of ordered rhythms, leading to an idealised order and a community of interests. Because of this and because of the enforced work, some forces are present and active in Russia which need most careful handling by the spiritual Hierarchy of our planet. These forces working in Russia are concerned with the magic of form whereas pure white magic is concerned only with the soul or with the subjective aspect, as it conditions the objective. The "black forces", so called, are nowhere rampant in Russia any more than in other parts of the world, but the Russian reaction and attitude to enforced rule and order has in it more of the magical seventh ray influence than is the case in other countries; Germany also enforced a standardised order and way of living but this was definitely submitted to the control of the black forces.

DN 54

Spain

Spain has a sixth ray ego and a seventh ray personality—thus reversing the forces which are expressing themselves through the Russian spirit. Spain, too, acts as a link in world adjustment but this time the link is between Europe and Africa, and in this capacity Spain has earlier served. It will be apparent to you also how inevitable has been the relationship between Spain and Russia and how the ideology of the latter country has influenced the national government. It will also be apparent why the battleground of two great ideologies—the Fascist and the Communistic—has been found inevitably in Spain. The triumph of the Fascist part has been equally inevitable from the start because of the egoic relation existing between Spain and Italy and also to the proximity of the two countries which has enabled the telepathic impress of Fascist idealism to be easily impressed upon the prepared and sensitive Spanish consciousness. As to the fanaticism, the natural cruelty, the fervent idealism, the arrogant pride and the religious and mystical quality of the Spanish character, they are obviously of sixth ray origin and are highly crystallised. The intense individualism of the people can be noted also as a definite part of their seventh ray personality equipment. Their spiritual motto: "I disperse the clouds", is indicative of the magical work for which Spain will eventually be responsible and sooner than is perhaps anticipated, thus balancing in that highly intelligent and individualistic country the field of scientific magic and the magical work of the Church of the future. This is a prophecy which lies at present too far ahead to be capable of verification, either in this generation or the next, but it is rooted in national characteristics and the law of probability.

DN 61-62

Seventh Ray Influences Via Planetary Rulers

Germany

Ray 7.—Ceremonial Order or Ritual, via Uranus. This affects the masses as a whole, as it is the hierarchical ruler and (because of their point of evolution) leads to their facile standardising and regimenting. The 7th ray also focusses or "grounds the first ray" and leads to the power direction which is given them.

DN 78

Great Britain

Ray 7.—Ceremonial Order or Organized Ritual, reaching our planet via Uranus and giving to the empire its grounded physical plane control over place and circumstance, its legal fundamentals, in cooperation with Libra, and its love of order and of rule, thus providing full expression for the first ray energies of the British Empire.

DN 84-85

The United States

Ray 7.—Order and Magic, via Uranus. This influence is inherited from the Atlantean world, which still rules the territorial aspect of the States, which is a remnant of old Atlantis. It is this that produces the many magical, spiritualistic and occult groups which flourish today in the States.

DN 90

CHAPTER SIX

THE SEVENTH RAY MANIFESTING THROUGH THE INDIVIDUAL

General Traits and Tendencies

Individualisation and the seventh ray

"The Blessed One sought the pathway into form, but held with firmness to the hand of the Magician. He sought to reconcile the Pilgrim, who was himself, to life in form. He sought to bring the world of disorder in which he found himself into some kind of order. He wandered far into the deepest depths and became immersed in chaos and disorder. He could not understand, yet still held to the hand of the Magician. He sought to bring about that order that his soul craved. He talked with all he met, but his bewilderment increased.

To the Magician thus he spoke: 'The ways of the Creator must be good. Behind all that which seems to be, must be a Plan. Teach me the purpose of it all. How can I work, immersed in deepest matter? Tell me the thing that I must do?'

The Magician said: 'Listen, O Worker in the furthest world, to the rhythm of the times. Note the pulsation in the heart of that which is divine. Retire into the silence and attune yourself unto the whole. Then venture forth. Establish the right rhythm; bring order to the forms of life which must express the Plan of Deity.'

For this Blessed One release is found in work. He must display his knowledge of the Plan by the sounding of those words which will evoke the Builders of the forms and thus create the new."

It might be of value, if here were summarized in more simple and less occult terms, the significance of the above esoteric stanzas, to express their true meaning in a few succinct and terse phrases. The stanzas are of no use unless they convey to the ray types among the students of this Treatise some useful meaning, whereby they can live more truly.

The individualised Spirit expresses itself through the various ray types in the following manner:—....

Ray Seven
> Black magic, or the use of magical powers for selfish ends.
> The power to "sit upon the fence" till the selfish values emerge.
> Disorder and chaos through misunderstanding of the Plan.
> The wrong use of speech to bring about chosen objectives.
> Untruth.
> Sex magic. The selfish perversion of soul powers,

> leading to

> White magic, the use of soul powers for spiritual ends.
> The identification of oneself with reality.
> Right order through right magic.
> Power to cooperate with the *Whole*.
> Understanding of the Plan.
> The magical work of interpretation.
> Manifestation of divinity.

EPII 38-43

It will not be possible for me to make clear the ray reactions to the final process which we have considered briefly, namely the stage in the liberation of the spirit which we call Identification. All that is possible, even in the case of Initiation, is to give the elementary stanzas which convey to accepted disciples some of the significance of the first initiation. As regards identification, the reactions of the illumined initiate are made available to his intelligence in symbolic form, but if these forms were described, they would be completely misunderstood. When the third initiation takes place and the wider open door looms before the initiate, he will then discover the meaning of that type of realisation which is here called (for lack of a better name) Identification.

EPII 44-45

Ray Seven
"The Angel of the Presence lifts one hand into the blue of heaven. He plunges deep the other into the sea of forms. Thus he connects the world of form and formless life. Heaven to earth he brings; earth into heaven. This the man, who stands before the Angel, knows.
He grasps the meaning of the painted sign which the Angel holds aloft. [Then follows a phrase which is incapable of translation into modern language. It signifies that complete merging which the mystic endeavours to express in terms of the "marriage in the heavens", and which has been wrongly twisted into the false teaching anent sex magic. This phrase, expressed by a painted symbol, symbolises complete unity between the outer and the inner, the objective and the subjective, between spirit and matter, and between the physical and the essential.]
The two are one. Naught more remains to grasp. The Word is manifest. The work is seen complete. The Whole is visioned. The magic work is wrought. Again the two are one. The Plan is served. No word need then be said."

These phrases are an attempt to express some of the realisations of the true initiate when he stands—at the third initiation—before the Angel and sees that Angel also pass away, so that naught is left but conscious knowledge and realisation. Although this statement may signify but little to us at present, it will, nevertheless, serve to demonstrate the futility of dealing with the secrets of the mysteries and with initiation through the medium of words. When this is better realised, the true work of the Masonic dramas will begin to measure up to the need.

This section expresses some of the basic emerging truths which will carry meaning to the senior disciples and the initiates of the world, who are battling, at this time, in the service of the Plan. They are present in the world at this time, and their work is bearing fruit, but they need at times the incentive of the future achievable glory to aid them to carry on.

This treatise is, therefore, somewhat abstruse and quite symbolical. It may appear difficult to comprehend, and it may mean little to some and nothing at all to others. If the disciples of the world are truly struggling and if they are applying practically the teaching given, as far as in them lies, they will find as time elapses, and their reason and intuition awaken, that such symbolic and abstruse statements become clearer and clearer, serving to convey the intended teaching. When this happens, the Angel of the Presence approaches ever closer, and lights the disciple on his way. The sense of separateness diminishes until, at last, light permeates the darkness, and the Angel dominates the life.

EPII 47-49

Egoic Ray. The Seven Directions of the Law of Repulse.

The effect of this Law of Repulse, as it works out in the world of discipleship and destroys that which hinders, sends the pilgrim hurrying back consciously along one of the seven rays that lead to the centre. This cannot be handled in detail here. Our present task is that of treading the Path of Probation or of Discipleship and of learning discipline, dispassion, and the other two necessities on the Way—discrimination and decentralisation. It is possible, nevertheless, to indicate the goal and point out the potency of the forces to which we shall be increasingly subjected as we pass—as some of us can so pass—on to the Path of Accepted Discipleship. This we will do in the form of seven stanzas which will give a hint (if one is an aspirant) of the technique to which one will be exposed; if one has passed further on the Way, they will give one a command which, as a disciple with spiritual insight one will obey, because one is awakened; if one is an initiate, they will evoke the comment: "This I know"....

The Direction of Ray VII.

"Under an arch between two rooms, the seventh Magician stood. One room was full of light and life and power, of stillness which was purpose and a beauty which was space. The other room was full of movement, a sound of great activity, a chaos without form, of work which had no true objective. The eyes of the Magician were fixed on chaos. He liked it not. His back was towards the room of vital stillness. He knew it not. The arch was tottering overhead....

He murmured in despair: 'For ages I have stood and sought to solve the problem of this room; to rearrange the chaos so that beauty might shine forth, and the goal of my desire. I sought to weave these colours into a dream of beauty, and to harmonise the many sounds. Achievement lacks. Naught but my failure can be seen. And yet I know there is a difference between that which I can see before my eyes and that which I begin to sense behind my back. What shall I do?'

Above the head of the Magician, and just behind his back, and yet within the room of ordered beauty, a magnet vast began to oscillate....It caused the revolution of the man, within the arch, which tottered to a future fall. The magnet turned him round until he faced the scene and room, unseen before....

Then through the centre of his heart the magnet poured its force attractive. The magnet poured its force repulsive. It reduced the chaos until its forms no longer could be seen. Some aspects of a beauty, unrevealed before, emerged. And from the room a light shone forth and, by its powers and life, forced the Magician to move forward into light, and leave the arch of peril."

EPII 166-72

Seventh Ray Technique of Integration...the integration with which we shall primarily deal...is that of the personality as it integrates into the whole of which it is a part, through service to the race and to the Plan. Bear in mind that these ray techniques are *imposed by the soul upon the personality after it has been somewhat integrated into a functioning unity* and is, therefore, becoming slightly responsive to the soul, the directing Intelligence....

EPII 351

Old Commentary
Ray Seven

" 'I seek to bring the two together. The plan is in my hands. How shall I work? Where lay the emphasis? In the far distance stands the One Who *Is*. Here at my hand is form, activity, substance, and desire. Can I relate these and fashion thus a form for God? Where shall I send my thought, my power the word that I can speak?'

'I, at the centre, stand, the worker in the field of magic. I know some rules, some magical controls, some Words of Power, some forces which I can direct. What shall I do? Danger there is. The task that I have undertaken is not easy of accomplishment, yet I love power. I love to see the forms emerge, created by my mind, and do their work, fulfill the plan and disappear. I can create. The rituals of the Temple of the Lord are known to me. How shall I work?'

'Love not the work. Let love of God's eternal Plan control your life, your mind, your hand, your eye. Work towards the unity of plan and purpose which must find its lasting place on earth. Work with the Plan, focus upon your share in that great work.'

The word goes forth from soul to form: 'Stand in the centre of the pentagram, drawn upon that high place in the East within the light which ever shines. From that illumined centre work. Leave not the pentagram. Stand steady in the midst. Then draw a line from that which is without to that which is within and see the Plan take form.'"

It is not possible to be more explicit than this. This great and powerful ray is now coming into manifestation and it brings new energies to man of so potent a nature that the disciples of today must move and work with care. They are literally handling fire. It is the children who are now coming into incarnation who will eventually work more safely and more correctly with these new potencies. There is much, however, to be done in the meantime, and the disciples upon this seventh ray can ponder on this formula and seek their own interpretation of it, endeavouring first of all to stand in the East, within the protection of the pentagram. As he realises the task to be carried out and the nature of the work to be done by the seventh ray worker, and appreciates the fact that it is the magical work of producing those forms on earth which will embody the spirit of God (and in our particular time, this necessitates the building of new forms), each seventh ray disciple will see himself as a relating agent, as the one who stands in the midst of the building processes, attending to his portion of the task. This, if really grasped and deeply considered will have the effect of producing alignment. The moment that this alignment is achieved, then let the disciple remember that it will mean a tremendous inflow of power, of energy from both the aligned points, from both directions, converging upon him, as he stands in the midway place. Ponder deeply upon this truth, for it is this fact which always evokes a seventh ray crisis. It will be obvious what this crisis is. If the man concerned is materially minded, selfishly ambitious and unloving, the inpouring energy will stimulate the personality nature and he will immediately be warring furiously with all that we mean by the instinctual, psychic, intellectual nature. When all these three are stimulated, the disciple is often for a time swung off the centre into a maelstrom of magical work of the lower kind—sex magic and many forms of black magic. He is glamoured by the beauty of his motive, and deceived by the acquired potency of his personality.

If, however, he is warned of the danger and aware of the possibility, he will stand steady at the centre within the mystical pentagram, and there *suffer* until the light in the East rises upon his darkness, discovering him still at the midway point. Then comes the revelation of the Plan, for this has ever to be the motivating power of the seventh ray disciple. He works on earth, upon the outer plane of manifestation, with the construction of those forms through which the divine will can express itself. In the field of religion, he works in collaboration with the second and sixth ray disciples. In the field of government he labours, building those forms which will enable the first ray activity to be expressed. In the field of business he cooperates with third ray energies and the executives of the Plan. In the field of science, he aids and assists the fifth ray workers. He is the expression of the builder, and the creator, bringing into outer manifestation God's Plan. He begins, however, with himself, and seeks to bring into expression the plan of his soul in his own setting and worldly situation. Until he can do this, he is unable to stand in the East within the pentagram.

It is occultly said that "the pentagram is open and a place of danger when the disciple knows not order within his own life, and when the ritual of the soul is not imposed and its rhythm not obeyed. The pentagram is closed when order is restored and the ritual of the Master is imposed". The writing goes on to say that "if the disciple enters through the open pentagram, he dies. If he passes over into the closed pentagram, he lives. If he transmutes the pentagram into a ring of fire, he serves the Plan."

EPII 375-78

On the Path of Return and in connection with the process of detachment, which marks the progress of the soul towards release and the ending of the period of appropriation, certain passages...give clearly the intended technique....

> Ray Seven:—"Let the builders cease their work. The Temple is completed. Let the soul enter into its heritage and from the Holy Place command all work to end. Then in the silence subsequent, let him chant forth the Word: `The creative work is over. I, the Creator, Am. Naught else remains but Me.'"

EPII 83-85

As I told you, and as I now repeat, the workers on all the rays are organised to take part in one supreme effort—an effort towards which the entire Christian era has been tending and for which it has been a preparation. The seventh and sixth rays are occupied with the work of government and with the task of producing a new synthesis, and thus the force of all the workers along those lines is combining with the energy of the first ray. The energies of the aspirants and disciples on the third and fifth rays are turned to the work of expanding the human consciousness, of bringing to light the hidden wonders of the universe, and of hastening the unfoldment of the latent powers in mankind. These powers, when awakened, will be extensions of many of the present senses and will admit man into that world which lies behind the veil of ignorance and matter.

You will note that so strenuous is the work of breaking down national group isolation and separativeness that it takes the united energies of three groups of workers to bring about the desired results. The seven groups of workers are organised therefore as follows:

1. In the department of politics....First, sixth and seventh rays.
2. In the department of religion....Second and fourth rays.
3. In the department of education....Third and fifth rays.

EPI 178

We are taught in the esoteric philosophy that seven great divine Emanations, Aeons or Spirits (in Whom we live and move and have our being) came forth from God at the time of the Creation. The same teaching can also be traced in the Holy Bible. Upon one or other of these seven Rays, the souls of all forms of life are to be found as well as the forms themselves. These seven rays produce the seven major psychological types. These seven rays or emanations are:

1. The first Ray of Will or Power. Many great world rulers are found on this ray, such as Julius Caesar.
2. The second Ray of Love-Wisdom. The Christ and the Buddha are to be found on this ray. It is the great teaching ray.
3. The third Ray of Active Intelligence. The mass of intelligent humanity are found on this ray.
4. The fourth Ray of Harmony through Conflict. Aspirants. Struggling, well-meaning people. Workers for unity emerge along this line.
5. The fifth Ray of Concrete Knowledge or Science. Scientists and people who are purely mental and governed only by the mind.

The Seventh Ray Manifesting Through the Individual 115

6. The sixth Ray of Devotion or Idealism. Many Christian people. Fanatics. Numbers of earnest Churchmen of all the world religions.
7. The seventh Ray of Ceremonial Order or Magic. Masons. Financiers. Great businessmen and organisers of all kinds. Executives are found with these energies in their equipment.

DINAI xiii-xiv

The Seventh Ray of Ceremonial Order or Magic

Special Virtues:

Strength, perseverance, courage, courtesy, extreme care in details, self-reliance.

Vices of Ray:

Formalism, bigotry, pride, narrowness, superficial judgments, self-opinion over-indulged.

Virtues to be acquired:

Realisation of unity, wide-mindedness, tolerance, humility, gentleness and love.

This is the ceremonial ray, the ray which makes a man delight in "all things done decently and in order", and according to rule and precedent. It is the ray of the high priest and the court chamberlain, of the soldier who is a born genius in organisation, of the ideal commissary general who will dress and feed the troops in the best possible way. It is the ray of the perfect nurse for the sick, careful in the smallest detail, though sometimes too much inclined to disregard the patients' idiosyncrasies and to try to grind them in the iron mill of routine.

It is the ray of form, the perfect sculptor, who sees and produces ideal beauty, of the designer of beautiful forms and patterns of any sort; but such a man would not be successful as a painter unless his influencing ray were the 4th. The combination of four with seven would make the very highest type of artist, form and colour both being in *excelsis*. The literary work of the seventh ray man would be remarkable for its ultra-polished style, and such a writer would think far more of the manner than of the matter in his work, but would always be fluent both in writing and speech. The seventh ray man will often be sectarian. He will delight in fixed ceremonials and observances, in great processions and shows, in reviews of troops and warships, in genealogical trees, and in rules of precedence.

The bad type of seventh ray man is superstitious, and such a man will take deep interest in omens, in dreams, in all occult practices, and in spiritualistic phenomena. The good type of the ray is absolutely determined to do the right thing and say the right word at the right moment; hence great social success.

In healing, the seventh ray man would rely on extreme exactness in carrying out orthodox treatment of disease. On him the practices of yoga would have no physical bad results.

He will approach the Path through the observance of rules of practice and of ritual, and can easily evoke and control the elemental forces.

EPI 210-11

Ray VII. This ray provides at this time an active and necessary grouping of disciples who are eager to aid the Plan. Their work lies naturally on the physical plane. They can organise the evoked ideal which will embody as much of the idea of God as the period and humanity can evidence and produce in form upon the earth. Their work is potent and necessary and calls for much skill in action. This is the ray that is coming into power. None of these ray participants in the hierarchical crusade today can really work without each other, and no group can carry on alone. The difference between the methods of the old age and that of the new can be seen expressed in the idea of leadership by one and leadership by a group. It is the difference between the impo-

The Seventh Ray Manifesting Through the Individual 117

sition of an individual's response to an idea upon his fellowmen and the reaction of a group to an idea, producing group idealism and focalising it into definite form, carrying forward the emergence of the idea without the dominance of any one individual. This is the major task today of the seventh ray disciple and to this end he must bend every energy. He must speak those Words of Power which are a group word, and embody the group aspiration in an organised *movement*, which, it will be noted is quite distinct from an organisation. A striking instance of the use of such a Word of Power being enunciated by a group has lately been given in the Great Invocation which has been used with marked effect. It should continue to be used, for it is the inaugurating mantram of the incoming seventh ray. This is the first time such a mantram has been brought to the attention of humanity.

All these rays work today for the carrying out of a specific group idea of seven Masters Who, through Their picked and chosen servers, are actively participating in the work which is the initiatory work of the seventh ray. It is also linked up with the incoming Aquarian influence....

EPII 145

The throat centre of the average integrated personality is governed by the third ray and is strongly energised by third ray energies (again seven in number), whilst the throat centre of the spiritual aspirant, of disciples and initiates below the third initiation is responding primarily to seventh ray influence, and this is peculiarly the case now as the seventh ray is in incarnation. The rays which are manifesting at any particular time affect powerfully all the other centres as well as the one through which they are normally expressing. This is a point oft forgotten.

TEL 137

The seventh ray person is faced with the difficulty of being able to create exceedingly clear-cut thoughtforms and the glamours, therefore, which control him are precise and definite, and, to him, all compelling. They rapidly crystallise, however, and die their own death .

GLA 222

Seventh Ray Glamours

> The glamour of magical work.
>
> The glamour of the relation of the opposites.
>
> The glamour of the subterranean powers.
>
> The glamour of that which brings together.
>
> The glamour of the physical body.
>
> The glamour of the mysterious and the secret.
>
> The glamour of sex magic.
>
> The glamour of the emerging manifested forces.

GLA 123

Instructions to Individual Members of the Tibetan's Seed Group

Discipleship in the New Age, Vols. I & II, contain two series of talks by the Tibetan to some members of his inner group, and also a series of personal instructions, given by him to a group of his disciples. The conflict in a disciple's life is found to lie in the fact that the ray of the soul and the ray of the integrated personality are posed against each other. At the same time, the emotional nature, mental equipment and physical brain are also controlled by some one or other of the rays and in this fivefold relationship lies hid much of the problem of the evolving human being. The Tibetan tells the members of his group which five rays condition them and students will learn much by a study of what he says. *Editors*

Your *soul* ray is the seventh, which would enable you to work with facility in the new world which is emerging into manifestation with such rapidity. It will aid you also in producing order and rhythm in your environment; in these days of turmoil and difficulty, every rhythmic centre is of value to us.

DINAI 646

...You have an interesting combination of ray energies with the ray of order, permitting of the physical establishment of relationship between soul and form strongly controlling you. This dominant energy should render your outer work effective upon the physical plane, if you will remember that esoterically the form nature is the vital etheric body, and this automatically and easily conditions the physical organised vehicle. When your work is not effective, brother of mine, what is the reason? Note that this seventh ray potency is concentrated in your personality, and when your second ray soul energy sweeps into prominence, the initial effect is oft to negate the activity of the personality. This is oft forgotten and is most confusing to the neophyte in its earlier manifestations. Later, the disciple learns from experiment and experience that all the rays are sub-rays of the great second ray. This you know theoretically, but that is different from the wisdom which comes from understanding as the result of action. Once this fact is grasped, you can begin to use all the forces in your equipment as the implements of loving service. Here lies your major technical lesson. Your line of least resistance is that of establishing relationship with the end in view of building a form. This is also the line of pure magic and—as you know—it can be either black or white. There are two modes of creative work: One mode is that which is implemented by seventh ray potency. This builds and creates within matter and within the periphery of the three worlds; it is exceedingly forceful when it is wielded through the medium of a seventh ray personality and a seventh ray physical body, as is the case with you. The other mode is that of the second ray, which is applied from *without* the three worlds and from soul levels; it works through radiation, magnetic appeal and coherent energy. Ponder on these two modes.

Through your ray energies, you are in a position to use both methods under the inspiration of the Ashram. The result should be most effective service and the steady growth of any work you may undertake for me and for the Ashram. You would find it useful to make a study of the relation of the second ray to the seventh, for there is a close creative reaction or impulsive interplay between the two, and one which you need to employ consciously.

DINAII 581-82

It is known to you that your major rays are the second and the seventh. The latter gives to you, if you can but understand it and choose to use it rightly, the power to take the light which is in you and in the pupil, and apply it to the enlightening of physical plane living, for the seventh ray is the ray controlling spirit-matter relationships.

DINAI 178

This seventh ray personality enables you to work actively in many ways upon the physical plane, bringing together the subjective reality and the outer form....

DINAI 344

I wonder whether you have sufficiently realised that for you to bring through the love of your soul is the line of least resistance, owing to the fact that your personality ray is the seventh ray—the ray of consummation, the ray of expressing adequately on the physical plane the form through which the soul—whose nature is love—can express itself. This is particularly easy also in your case because the ray of your physical body is also the seventh. The line of descent, therefore, for the form building energy is direct. To this again you can add the fact that your

The Seventh Ray Manifesting Through the Individual 121

personality vehicles are on the fifth, the sixth, and the seventh rays; these follow each other in sequential order, producing again a direct channel. You should consequently (if you are truly to understand the mechanism through which your soul has to function) make a much closer study of the seventh ray. It is also the incoming ray for the next immediate cycle. A knowledge of the ray influences, techniques, mechanics and objectives will be ascertained by disciples in whom these rays are pronouncedly manifesting.

DINAII 574

In reference to the work of fusion at which you must arrive in connection with your bodily forces and your soul energy, I would call your attention to the fact that your soul energy is focussed in your physical equipment, thus bringing together the energy of your soul and the force of your seventh ray brain. There is, consequently, a direct alignment between soul and brain and this must be deepened, understood and utilised.

DINAI 171

I suggest that you take until next May before coming to your final decision. I have asked a member of another group in my Ashram to do your work in the meantime. I am therefore assigning you no work, and you are regarded as temporarily suspended from the group. I ask naught of you but that you reconsider your decision from the angle of group good and group progress, and from that of your group brothers, and not solely from the angle of what seems best to you yourself and your own comfort, and your own so-called freedom. Infer not from this that I regard your decision as a selfish one. I know what it has cost you. It is, nevertheless, based on feeling, and feeling is seldom a true indication of right action. I seek only to give you the time to think. I would remind you as you seek decision that your soul is on the seventh ray and that you are working through a first ray personality. Hence, my brother, your problem. A mystic of wide consciousness with a powerful personality ray and with a soul vibration in line with the New Age, seeking to impose upon the personality the rhythm of a "ceremonial order and organisation". I would ask you to bear in mind that group work involves sacrifice and oft the doing of that which might not be preferred and which might not—from the personality angle—be the easier way out and the easier activity. The choice, however, rests with you and the thoughts of the group must be kept away from your decision, so that you can make it freely and unhampered. The group must then abide by your decision.

DINAI 290

You are a second ray soul and have a seventh ray personality.

This seventh ray personality enables you to work actively in many ways upon the physical plane, bringing together the subjective reality and the outer form. Your feeling that there is in you indication of a fifth ray activity is due to the fact that it was your personality ray in your last life and is, for you, the line of least resistance therefore.

DINAI 344

If you can grasp clearly the implications of what I now seek to tell you, you will make real progress. I shall leave you to find out for yourself what the implications are. You are at a point in your development where—unless you emerge into a more mental type of realisation—you will crystallise into a high grade astral magician and arrest your own true development for this life. Three things I would like to point out to you in this connection:

1. You spend the greater part of your subjective life upon the astral plane.

The Seventh Ray Manifesting Through the Individual 123

2. You endeavour—largely unconsciously—to work as an astral magician works, using words to bring life and form together. You do not use the Word.
3. The work you do is done on astral levels and not from soul levels so that the Word of Power which the soul would use is stepped down to the many, many words the astral magician finds necessary. Your emphasis is now upon the form and not upon the spirit aspect.

This is due to two things: First, the fact that your personality ray is the seventh and you have likewise a seventh ray brain. Secondly, you brought this tendency over from a previous life; your task has been to transcend it all and free yourself from all magical work of every kind until you are established in soul consciousness. But at present you love this type of thing and believe that all you contact is a reality. As long as this is the case, *your soul life is blocked at astral levels.*

Another difficulty, growing out of this, is the fact that because of this astral impasse, your soul is focussed in the astral body. It can get no further into expression, i.e., on the physical plane, on account of the glamour which surrounds you. Your personality energy is focussed in the mental body. This brings the influence of the magical seventh ray to bear upon your mind, so that you are caught by glamour in two directions. Your brain being also an expression of seventh ray force facilitates this work of magic.

Until, my brother, you are polarised in the soul, you are playing with fire and the magical work of the astral plane is full of danger for you. Even your intense interest in Masonry is for this life unwise, for the Masonic Work is magical work, being a reflection of the processes of initiation whereby the power of the spirit and the power of substance are brought together through the *"magical work of the soul"*.

DINAI 635-36

...Your whole problem is tied up with your ray qualities, for you are on the second ray where your soul is concerned, whilst you function through a first ray personality. You have, however, a strong seventh ray development because that was the ray upon which your personality was found in your last incarnation. Hence your capacity to organise (which is of the seventh ray) and the ease with which you handle detail (which is a second ray characteristic).

DINAI 497-98

This seventh ray is a ray of a dual activity, because through its means the energy of the soul and of the personality can be brought consciously into relation, and this more easily than on the other rays, once the disciple is freed from glamour. Thus there can be built a true expression of the life content—from the angle of a long soul experience. This may sound to you somewhat ambiguous, but the statement is by no means as vague as it appears. It should provide you with ideas for reflection.

DINAII 670

...the healing ray above all others, is the second ray. There are two major healing rays among the seven. They are the second and the seventh. The success of all healing enterprise, therefore, depends upon the ability of the group members to work at will and on demand, under the influence of their souls....

If you will study your rays, my brother, you will note that you are eminently equipped to heal, for you have two streams of second ray energy flowing through you and also two streams of seventh ray energy. This makes for power in healing.

DINAI 641

The seventh ray in your personality and physical body gives you the desire to use your hands and it determines your life work, because the hands are the agents of the magician and you are most definitely upon the Path of the White Magician.

DINAI 352

As you have already guessed, your *physical body* is on the seventh ray. Hence your Masonic opportunity and your ability to organise and rule. I would remind you all that when the statement is made that the physical body is upon the seventh ray, it means that the atoms of the brain, in particular, are coloured and motivated by seventh ray energy. So it is with all the rays upon which a physical vehicle may be found. This provides a definite opportunity to those so constituted at this time in connection with the seventh ray, as it is coming into influence so rapidly. At the same time it provides a problem—that unending problem of the balancing of forces which is the major task of the initiate or of those in training for initiation....

DINAI 168

Your *physical body* is on the seventh Ray of Ceremonial Order or Magic, and hence your interest in spiritualism, for one thing, and hence also your choice of a life profession, for another. Hence also the facility with which you could establish and hold a steady contact between soul-mind-brain....

DINAI 549-50

Your *physical body* is upon the seventh ray and this makes for integration and for efficiency....

DINAI 583

Your *physical body* is upon the seventh ray, and this will be easily apparent to you, accounting, as it does, for your interest in music, ritual, psycho-analysis. The goal of all these three methods of expression is to bring together and relate harmoniously the soul and the form, which is the major task of the seventh ray upon the seventh or physical plane....

DINAI 640

Your *physical body* is on the seventh ray, which gives you a sense of the relationship between spirit and matter, between soul and body and enables you, if so you will, to be a constructive agent in magical work....

DINAI 133

The *physical body* is of the seventh ray type but it is so controlled by your fourth ray personality that—in a most peculiar sense—it has little life of its own. It is negative to an amazing extent and this again constitutes a definite problem....

DINAI 152

Your *physical body* is upon the seventh ray. This should give you facile expression of your personality purpose upon the physical plane....

DINAI 350

...Your personality force is focussed in your seventh ray brain. This gives you the power to plan, to organise, and also the power to give form to ideas. Ponder also on this.

DINAI 668

Your *physical body* is on the seventh Ray of Ceremonial Order or Magic; here is to be found the source of much of your ill-health. The seventh plane is the plane upon which spirit must express itself. It is the receptacle of spiritual energy. Your physical vehicle and medium of expression is of such a sensitive and refined nature and so frail a receptacle that your life problem is to handle wisely the spiritual energy which seeks to pour through. This constitutes a very real problem which you have faced for years and must continue to face.

DINAI 438

If you will study your ray combinations, you will note that you have only one of your ray energies along the line of the first ray—that is the ray of the seventh type of energy. All your other rays are related to the great Second Ray of Love-Wisdom. This necessarily constitutes a problem until you remember that the seventh ray is the ray of interlude—an interlude and a ray which becomes active when the attractive, magnetic work of the building rays is ready to precipitate into the phenomenal world and bring about—under the Law of Ritual and of Divine Ceremonial—new phases of work. These are initiated in the silence of the process of abstraction, released when the interlude of tension has completed its work, and become effective when the interlude of recognition has made a new refocussing possible....

I am pleased that you are following along the line of your second ray energy, and are occupied with seventh ray activity; that means that, inspired by the sense of unity which is inherent in the soul, you are working on the physical plane (the point of expression for the seventh ray) and bringing spirit and matter together. Remember always that this ray which is again coming into cyclic manifestation is the one that relates the new and incoming spiritual energy and the substance or matter aspect which will respond to it, utilise it and eventually give it due form. Know therefore clearly what it is you are attempting to do.

DINAII 454-57

CHAPTER SEVEN

ESOTERIC HEALING AND THE SEVENTH RAY

The seventh ray technique

Energy and force must meet each other and thus the work is done. Colour and sound in ordered sequence must meet and blend and thus the work of magic can proceed. Substance and spirit must evoke each other and, passing through the centre of the one who seeks to aid, produce the new and good. The healer energises thus with life the failing life, driving it forth or anchoring it yet more deeply in the place of destiny. All seven must be used and through the seven there must pass the energies the need requires, creating the new man who has for ever been and will for ever be, and either here or there.

In this technique you have the clue to them all, for the work of the seventh ray healer is to bring together the life and the substance which will take the place of the substance which is diseased and bring new life to aid the recovery. The glory of life lies in consummation and in emergence. This is the prime task and the prime reward of all true healers. It is this technique of attraction and substitution which will be brought to a fine point of scientific expression in the coming new age wherein the seventh ray will dominate our planet, producing that which is new and needed and determining the coming culture, civilisation and science.

EH 712-13

The Seventh Ray Cause of Inharmony and Disease

VII. "The Great One gathered to Himself His forces and affirmed His intention to create. He created that which is outer and can be seen. He saw His creations and liked

Esoteric Healing and the Seventh Ray

them not and so withdrew His attention; then the creations He had made died and disappeared. He had no lasting success and saw naught but failure as He travelled on the outer path of life. He comprehended not the need of forms. To some He gave an over-plus of life, to some too little; and so both kinds died and failed to show the beauty of the Lord Who gave them life but failed to give them understanding. He knew not then that love sustains."

The effects of this ray force are most peculiar and will be a great deal more prevalent than heretofore, as this ray is now coming into power. It is this energy which is largely responsible for infections and contagious diseases. The keynote of the work of the seventh ray is to bring together life and matter upon the physical plane. This, however, when viewed from the angle of imperfection, is a bringing together (if you can understand the implications) of Life, the lives and the general livingness of the creative process. This is symbolised by the promiscuity and the endless moving interplay of all life within all lives. The result is therefore the activity of all germs and bacteria within the medium which will best nurture them.

EH 303-04

Effect on the Physical Body

...The disciple is learning to lift the energies, gathered from the lower centres, into the solar plexus and from that centre into the heart centre, thus bringing about a refocussing of the energies above the diaphragm instead of putting the emphasis below. This leads frequently to profound complications, because—from the personality angle—the solar plexus centre is the most potent, being the clearing house for the personality forces. It is that process of decentralisation and "elevation" of the lower consciousness to the higher which produces the main difficulties to which the disciple is subjected. It is this process also which is going on in the world as a whole today, causing the appalling disruption of human affairs, culture and civilisation. The entire focus of humanity's consciousness is being changed; the selfish life (characteristic of the man centred in his desires and consequently in the solar plexus centre) is giving place to the decentralised life of the man who is unselfish (centred in the Self or soul), aware of his relationships and responsibility to the Whole and not to the part. This sublimation of the lower life into the higher is one of deepest moment to the individual and to the race. Once the individual disciple, and humanity as well, symbolising the world disciple, have mastered the process of transference in this respect, we shall see the new order of individual service and of world service established, and therefore the coming in of the awaited new order.

Of all these processes, the circulation of the blood stream is the symbol, and the clue to the establishment of the world order lies hid in this symbology—free circulation of all that is needed to all parts of the great framework of humanity. The blood is the life, and free interchange, free sharing, free circulation of all that is required for right human living will characterise the world to be. Today these conditions do not exist, the body of humanity is diseased and its internal life disrupted. Instead of free circulation between all parts of the life aspect, there has been separation, blocked channels, congestion and stagnation. It has needed the terrific crisis of the present to arouse humanity to its diseased condition, to the extent of the evil which is now discovered to be so great, and the diseases of the "blood of humanity" (symbolically understood) so severe that only the most drastic measures—pain, agony, despair and terror—can suffice to establish a cure.

Healers would do well to remember this, and to have in mind that disciples and all good men and aspirants share in this universal disease of humanity which must take its

Esoteric Healing and the Seventh Ray

toll psychologically or physically or both. The trouble is of ancient origin and of long established habit and inevitably affects the physical vehicle of the soul. Exemption from the effects of human ills is no indication of spiritual superiority. It might simply indicate what one of the Masters has called "the depths of spiritual selfishness and self-satisfaction". The initiate of the third degree can hold himself exempt, but this is only because he has completely freed himself from glamour and no aspect of the personality life has any further power over him. All the ray types are equally subjected to these particular problems. The seventh ray, however, is more susceptible to the problems, difficulties and diseases incident to the blood stream than are any of the other ray types. The reason is that this is the ray which has to do with the expression and manifestation of life upon the physical plane and with the organisation of the relationship between spirit and matter into form. It is concerned therefore today, as it seeks to create the new order, with free circulation and with a consequently intended freedom of humanity from the ills and problems of the past. This is of interest to remember, and students would find it helpful at this time, if they want to cooperate intelligently with the happenings of the day, to collect and study all that I have written about the seventh Ray of Ceremonial Order and Magic.

EH 127-29

Healers on the second, third and fifth rays use more generally the mode of laying on of hands or *magnetic healing*. This term applies to the direct act of laying on of hands upon the patient's physical body, and not to the action of the hands in the second method, when the hands are immersed in the etheric body of the patient and are definitely working in etheric matter. Healers on the first, fourth and seventh rays use the mode of "hand immersion", as it is sometimes called. The sixth ray healer is rare and is successful only when highly developed; he will then use both methods interchangeably.

EH 650

Today we are watching the passing out of the sixth ray energy and the growing power and activity of the seventh ray. The energy which is withdrawing itself from our planet in one of the cyclic crises has for centuries expressed itself through the planetary solar plexus and also, as might be inferred, through the solar plexus centre of the average aspirant. This has led to much of the digestive difficulties, plus the emotional problems (and are they not closely related) from which the majority of people have suffered in this age and generation. The intense one-pointed attitude, the fanatical state of mind, the sacrifice of the personal life to the sensed ideal have all brought about a dangerous condition in those organs of the body which lie below the diaphragm. This should be remembered.

The seventh ray, working as it does through the centre at the base of the spine, will in time have a peculiar effect upon the entire circulatory system, for this basic centre is connected with the life-force and, as you know, the "blood is the life". It works with the highest centre in the body and is therefore related to the entire problem of the polarities. It is consequently one of the factors which will increase the difficulties connected with the various psychological "cleavages" with which we have earlier dealt. It concerns the human triplicity of spirit-soul-body, the duality of soul and personality and the major aspects of Deity, spirit and matter, as well as the many groupings of the pairs of opposites with which the mystic is so constantly concerned and which he has eventually to resolve into a unity. The recognition of this will make clear how complex are the problems and the possibilities arising out of the stimu-

Esoteric Healing and the Seventh Ray 133

lation which will be felt as the "will to circulate, the will to relate and the will to express" makes its presence felt with the manifestation of the seventh ray. This force, as far as the individual is concerned, will play upon the centre at the base of the spine, arousing it into a hitherto unknown activity. These aspects of the will life are fortunately for humanity far from full development, but much of the present world confusion and the swing between the expressed extremes, are to be attributed to the play of these new forces. Much of the untimely and over-emphasised expression of the *Will* aspect of certain nations and individuals is connected with the coming into manifestation of this seventh ray and the passing out of the old. The problem is greatly increased by the fact that there is apparently a pronounced affinity between the fanatical idealistic will of the sixth ray—which is crystallised, directed, unwavering, emotional emphasis—and the will force of the untrained magical worker who is influenced by seventh ray energy, working through the centre at the base of the spine.

EPII 622-23

In conclusion I would like to tell you the reasons I am refraining from more detailed information and from a clear analysis of the wording of these ancient formulas of healing. Apart from the reason, earlier stated, that men are not yet ready to be given explicit instructions, for the time being anything I might say would appear to you puerile. That is the curious word which seems to be descriptive of possible immediate reaction. We are on the verge of entering a new era in scientific unfoldment, owing to the discovery of how to release the energy of the atom. Not even the scientists responsible for the discovery have the faintest idea of the far-reaching effects of this momentous happening. From the angle of our subject and the theme of this volume, an entirely new language related to energy and force is already in the making; the use of the discovery in the handling of disease will, in almost the immediate future (from the occult angle) be regarded as little short of miraculous.

This discovery of atomic liberation has been brought about by the activity of the first ray in relation to the incoming seventh ray and has its analogous situation in the liberation of the Master at the fifth initiation (when the door of the tomb bursts wide open) and in the act of dying, when the imprisoned soul finds release. In the light of future scientific happenings, these ancient techniques will become much clearer, and in the meantime any explanation of their true "energetic import" would be meaningless. The new and coming terminology will throw light on the ancient formulas, and in time you will see how much can be conveyed to the intelligent healer of that new generation by what seems to you both disappointing, without use or significance, and needlessly abstruse.

In this interim period between the past and that which is on its way, it is not easy for even a Master of the Wisdom to speak or teach, particularly in connection with the theme of healing. The physical body is not yet generally recognised as an electrical unit; its nature as pure atomic energy is not yet realised; the fact of the energy body, the etheric vehicle, is not at this time recognised in the teachings of the modern medical schools, though the fact has been discussed; the explosive nature of energy, when in contact with force, or of the soul in relation to substance, is completely unknown or veiled in mystical language. Until such time as the new scientific formulas and the new approach (which the discovery of the release of atomic energy has made possible) have become more generally understood, are a familiar subject of discussion and couched in familiar language, the coming science of healing must remain behind a veil of unsuitable language and hidden by inappropriate words.

This fact, as I have oft told you, handicaps all new presentations of truth; the language of the electrical engineer or of the automobile draftsman, for instance, would have been entirely meaningless to the average man a hundred years ago. So it is with the new themes and the great discoveries which are on their way and which will eventually affect every department of human life, including the Art of Healing.

EH 713-14

CHAPTER EIGHT

MEDITATION - THE SEVENTH RAY IMPACT

The occult form

We studied...the method whereby the mystic attains union, and outlined very briefly the path whereby he attempts to reach his goal. Today we will outline as briefly the course taken by the occultist, and his type of meditation, contrasting it with that of the mystic, and pointing out later how the two have to merge and their individual elements be fused into one.

The line of *form* is, for the occultist, the line of least resistance, and incidentally I might here interpolate a thought. The fact being admitted, we may therefore look with some certainty at this time for a rapid development of occult knowledge, and for the appearance of some true occultists. By the coming in of the seventh ray, the Ray of Form or Ritual, the finding of the occult path, and the assimilation of occult knowledge is powerfully facilitated. The occultist is at first occupied more with the form through which the Deity manifests than with the Deity Himself, and it is here that the fundamental difference between the two types is at first apparent. The mystic eliminates or endeavours to transcend *mind* in his process of finding the Self. The occultist, through his intelligent interest in the forms which veil the Self and by the employment of the *principle of mind* on both its levels, arrives at the same point. He recognises the sheaths that veil. He applies himself to the study of the laws that govern the manifested solar system. He concentrates on the objective, and in his earlier years may at times overlook the value of the subjective. He arrives eventually at the central life by the elimination, through conscious knowledge and control, of sheath after sheath. He meditates upon form until the

Meditation - The Seventh Ray Impact

form is lost sight of, and the creator of the form becomes all in all.

LOM 151

The Day of Opportunity

The question might here be asked wherein this information is of value to the student. In illustration of this it would be wise if students would ponder the significance of the coming in of the present Ray of Ceremonial Law or Magic. It is the ray that deals with the building forces of nature, that concerns itself with the utilisation of the form intelligently by the life aspect. It is largely the ray of executive work, with the object of building, co-ordinating and producing cohesion in the four lower kingdoms of nature. It is distinguished largely by the energy which manifests itself in ritual, but this word ritual must not be narrowed down to its present use in connection with Masonic, or religious ritual. Its application is far wider than this, and includes the methods of organisation which are demonstrated in all civilised communities, such as in the world of commerce and of finance, and the great business organisations everywhere to be seen. Above all, its interest lies for us in the fact that it is the ray which brings opportunity to the occidental races, and through the medium of this life force of executive organisation, of government by rule and order, by rhythm and by ritual, will come the time wherein the occidental races (with their active, concrete mind, and their vast business capacity) can take initiation—an initiation, we must remember, upon a ray which is temporarily recognised as a major ray. A large number of the initiates and those who have obtained adeptship in the last cycle, have been orientals and those in Hindu bodies. This cycle has been dominated by the sixth ray, which is just passing out, and the two preceding. In the preservation of equilibrium the time now comes when a period of attainment by occidentals will be seen, and this upon a ray suited to their type of mind. It is interesting to note that the oriental type attains its objective through meditation, with a modicum of executive organisation and ritual, and that the occidental will achieve largely through the organisation which lower mind produces, and a type of meditation of which intense business concentration might be considered an illustration. The one-pointed application of the mind by a European or American business man might be regarded as a type of meditation. In the purification of motive lying back of this application will come, for the occidental, his day of opportunity.

IHS 182-83

You will see, therefore, that when the real occult work is begun, the method may differ—and will necessarily differ—in the east and in the west, but the goal will be the same. It must be borne in mind, for instance, that a meditation that would aid the development of an oriental, might bring danger and disaster to his western brother. The reverse would also be the case. But always the goal will be the same. Forms may be individual or collective, mantrams may be chanted by units or by groups, different centres may be the object of specialised attention, yet the results will be identical. Danger arises when the occidental bases his endeavour on rules that suffice for the oriental, as has at times been so wisely pointed out. In the wisdom of the Great Ones this danger is being offset. Different methods for different races, diverse forms for those of various nationalities, but the same wise guides on the inner planes, the same great Hall of Wisdom, the same Gate of Initiation, admitting all into the inner sanctuary....

In concluding this subject, I seek to give a hint:—The seventh Ray of Ceremonial Law or Order (the ray now coming into power) provides for the occidental what has long been the privilege of the oriental. Great is the day of opportunity, and in the sweeping onward of this seventh force comes the needed impetus that may—if rightly grasped—drive to the Feet of the Lord of the World the dweller in the occident.

LOM 113-14

Now I would emphatically point out to you the fact that all that I now impart is a portion of a tentative plan, which has in view the hastening of the evolution of the higher mind, and the bringing under control of the bodies of men, through the power of the God within. This plan has been drawn up in view of the crying need of a world in which the mental equipment of men is increasing out of all proportion to their emotional balance and to their physical equipment. The rapid advance of knowledge, the spreading of the educational system which brings the product of many minds into the environment of the very poor, the ability of all to read and write in such a country as America or among the other Anglo-Saxon races, has been the cause of a very real (I might almost say an unexpected) problem arising to confront the Great Ones.

Mental development when paralleled by emotional stability and a strong healthy body is the aim for all. But now you have mental development paralleled by an unstable astral and a weak, underfed, badly raised physical. Hence disorder, lack of balance, the clouding of the vision and disproportionate discussion. Lower mind, instead of being a means to an end and a weapon for use, is in fair way of being a ruler and a tyrant, preventing the play of the intuition and shutting out the abstract mind.

Hence the Masters, if it can in any way be accomplished, purpose a movement that has in view the harnessing of the lower mind through the instrumentality of the people themselves. With this object in view They plan to utilise the incoming Ray of Ceremonial Law or Organisation, and the period immediately co-incident or following the coming of the Great Lord, to start these schools (in a small inconspicuous way at first) and bring to the consciousness of men everywhere the following four fundamentals:—

  a. The evolutionary history of man *from the mental side.*
  b. The septenary constitution of the macrocosm and the microcosm.
  c. The laws governing man's being.
  d. The method of occult development.

A beginning has already been made...through the various schools at present extant....All these are the beginnings of the plan. When they are firmly grounded, when they are working smoothly and with public recognition, and when the world of men is being somewhat coloured by them and their *subjective* emphasis, when they are producing scholars and workers, politicians and scientists and educational leaders who make their impress on their environment, then mayhap will come the time for the founding in exoteric fashion of the true occult school. By that I mean that if the earlier schools and colleges do their work satisfactorily they will have demonstrated to the world of men that the subjective is the true reality and that the lower is but the stepping stone to the higher. This subjective reality being universally admitted will, therefore, permit of the founding of a chain of inner schools...that will be publicly recognised. This will never at any time obviate the necessity for always having an esoteric and secret section, for always there will be certain truths and facts of dangerous import to the uninitiated; but what I seek to point out is that the mysteries will eventually be admitted as facts for universal recognition and for universal aim and goal. They will be prepared for and entered from schools that definitely undertake, under expert guidance, to train noviatites for the mysteries.

Such schools have existed before and in the turning of the wheel again they will be in manifestation.

You ask, when? That depends on humanity itself and on all of you who work with faith and aspiration at the beginnings of the plan.

H.P.B. laid the foundation stone of the first school in this particular lesser cycle (which is nevertheless a relatively important one, being an outgrowth of the fifth root-race, the efflorescence of the fifth principle). This is the keystone. The work proceeds in the founding, as aforesaid, of the various schools, and mental science also has its place. It will go forward as desired if each one who is now under occult training strains every nerve and bends every effort to the work in hand. If all that is possible is done, when the Great Lord comes with His Masters the work will receive a still further impetus, and will gradually expand and grow till it becomes a power in the world. Then will come the day of the occult schools that will definitely train men for initiation.

LOM 299-301

The ray on which a man's causal body is found, the egoic ray, should determine the type of meditation. Each ray necessitates a different method of approach, for the aim of all meditation is union with the divine. At this stage, it is union with the spiritual Triad, that has its lowest reflection on the mental plane. Let me illustrate briefly:....

When the egoic ray is the seventh or *Ray of Ceremonial Law or Magic*, the method is that of the glorification and comprehension of form in approach. As said earlier, the goal of all the meditation practices is approach to the divine within each one, and, through that, approach to the Deity Himself.

The method, therefore, is the bringing under law, order and rule, of every act of the life in all the three bodies, and the building within the causal body of an expanding form that results in the shattering of that body. It is the building of the Shrine under certain rules into a dwelling place for the Shekinah, and when the spiritual light flames forth, the Temple of Solomon rocks, reels and disintegrates. It is the study of the law and the consequent comprehension by the man of how that law is wielded and why; it is then the definite application of that law to the body of causes so as to render it needless and thus effect its shattering. Emancipation is the result, and the man frees himself from the three worlds. Many occultists are coming in on this ray at this time to continue the liberating process. It is the method that leads a man to liberation through the understanding and the intelligent application of the law to his own life, and to the ameliorating of conditions in the body of humanity, thus making the man a server of his race.

LOM 15-19

Until now we have dealt more with the personal aspects of meditation, and have considered the two types that are practically universal and fundamental, having studied briefly, (a) Meditation as followed by the mystic, and (b) Meditation as pursued by the occultist.

We have largely generalised and have not in any way attempted to enter into particulars. It is neither desirable at this stage nor proper. At a certain point in meditation, nevertheless, when the pupil has made the desired progress and covered certain specific stages and attained certain objectives (which attainment can be ascertained by a review of the pupil's causal body) and when a foundation of right living has been laid which neither storms nor attack will be liable easily to upset or destroy, the Teacher may impart to the earnest pupil instructions whereby he can build in mental matter and under definite rules, forms that will lead to specific actions and reactions. These forms will be imparted gradually, and at times the pupil (this especially at first) may not be in the least conscious of the results achieved. He will obey the orders, say the imparted words, or work through the outlined formulas, and the results attained may do their work even though the pupil is unconscious of the fact. Later—especially after initiation, as the subtler faculties come into activity, and the centres are rotating in fourth dimensional order—he may be aware of the effects of his meditation on the emotional and mental planes.

Results never concern us. Strict obedience to the law, and steady adherence to the rules laid down, with skill in action aimed at are the part of the wise pupil. The effects then are sure, and carry no karma with them.

...Let us take up each of the forms in order, but first I would give a warning. I do not intend to outline forms, or to give specific instructions as to how the results indicated may be achieved. That will be done later, but when, it is not possible to say. So much depends upon the work done during the next seven years, or on the group karma, also on the progress made, not only by the human hierarchy, but by the deva or angel evolution as well. The secret of it all lies hid in the seventh Ceremonial Ray, and the hour for the next step onward will be given by the seventh Planetary Logos, working in conjunction with three Great Lords, especially with the Lord of the third department.

LOM 154-56

Building the Antahkarana

Until the stage of projection is reached, the methods employed by all disciples on all rays are identical. Their intention is one, and they all have to attain the same measure of tension and of preparation for the construction of the bridge by gathering the needed energy from two sources—the personality and the soul. By this focussing and its resultant tension, by thus evoking the Spiritual Triad and starting the dual process of building from both ends of the bridge (if such a phrase is possible and permissible), the work goes forward uniformly. The use of the creative imagination is now called forth and this forms the second stage. This presents a real difficulty for the first ray and the seventh ray aspirants. Neither type can with facility organise the material energy, orient energy currents, and see their objective clearly in the mind's eye pictorially. It is a process which is profoundly difficult for them. It must, however, in some way be done, because the use of the visual imagination is an essential factor in the building process and one of the major means of focussing prior to projection.

RI 501-02

It is along the antahkarana that the force used by the initiate must pour, and according to the nature of the work to be done will be the particular strand or thread of the rainbow bridge which the initiate employs. There are four veils of maya, constructed necessarily of seven forces, and these produce the factual and phenomenal aspect (in time and space) of the Great Illusion, in its three forms of *illusion, glamour* and *maya*. There are seven points of energy through which different aspects of the force needed to produce the desired effects within the veils of maya can flow, and these correspond to the seven ray types or qualities. But the major type of energy with which the initiate works upon the physical plane is the seventh, the ray or energy of ritual, of ceremony, of order and of law. The work done within the veils is one of rearrangement and the ordination and coordination of the forces, present as existent maya; this must provide, in time and space, the forms through which the plans of the Hierarchy can materialise, the souls of all forms can be subjected to the needed experience, and so progress towards the fulfilment of the will of God.

RI 183

Word of Power
    Ray Seven . . . Ceremonial Law or Order
        "THE HIGHEST AND THE LOWEST MEET"

RI 518

CHAPTER NINE

THE SEVENTH RAY AND INITIATION

Initiation 1. The Birth at Bethlehem. Ray VII
The Energy of Order or Ceremonial Magic

First of all, let us consider the type of energy which the seventh ray expresses and wherein lies its potency and efficacy, from the angle of initiation. As we study these initiations and their conditioning rays, we will divide our ideas into three parts:

1. The type of energy and its quality in relation to the processes of the particular initiation with which it is associated.
2. Its effect upon humanity, regarding humanity as a world disciple.
3. The stimulating nature of the energy as it expresses itself:

   a. In the three aspects of the initiate's nature—mental, astral and physical.

   b. Through the soul-infused personality, the initiate "in good standing"—a phrase of the deepest occult implication.

At this particular time in world history, seventh ray energy is of a growing potency because it is the new and incoming ray, superseding the sixth ray which has for so long held sway. When we speak of ray energy we are in reality considering the quality and the will-purpose aspect of a certain great Life to Whom we give the name "Lord of a Ray". You will find much about these Ray Lords in the earlier volumes of *A Treatise on the Seven Rays*. His divine intention, will, purpose, or the determined projection of His mind, creates a radiation or stream of energy which—according to type and quality—plays upon all forms of

The Seventh Ray and Initiation

manifested life within our planetary ring-pass-not. These Lords of the Rays are the creating and sustaining energies which implement the Will of the planetary Logos. They cooperate with Him in the defining and the expression of His supreme purpose. Their radiating emanations are cyclically objectified and are cyclically withdrawn. As they radiate forth into the three worlds, the impacting energies produce changes, disturbances, progress and unfoldment; they create the needed new forms and vitalise and qualify that through which the immediate divine intention is expressing itself; they intensify both the quality and the receptivity of consciousness.

At other times, during the process of being withdrawn "to their own place", they cause the fading out or the dying of form aspects, of institutions, and the "organising organisms" (to use a peculiar phrase); they therefore produce cycles of destruction and of cessation and thus make room for those new forms and life expressions which an incoming ray will produce. It has been the gradual withdrawing of the sixth Ray of Idealism and of one-pointed Devotion which has been responsible for the ferment, crystallisation, destruction, death and cleavages of the past century; old things are passing away as the Lord of the sixth Ray withdraws His attention, and therefore His energy; His radiation is today no longer centred or focussed in the life of the three worlds. Simultaneously, the energy and radiation of the Lord of the seventh Ray are becoming steadily more powerful in the three worlds.

This incoming of a ray always produces an intensified period of initiatory activity, and this is the case today. The major effect, as far as humanity is concerned, is to make possible the presentation of thousands of aspirants and applicants for the first initiation; men on a large scale and in mass formation can today pass through the experience of the Birth Initiation. Thousands of human beings can experience the birth of the Christ within themselves and can realise that the Christ life, the Christ nature and the Christ consciousness are theirs. This "new birth" initiation of the human family will take place in Bethlehem, symbolically understood, for Bethlehem is the "house of bread"—an occult term signifying physical plane experience. These great initiations, implemented by the ray energies, must be registered in the physical brain and recorded by the waking consciousness of the initiate, and this must be the case in this amazing period wherein—for the first time since humanity appeared on Earth—there can take place a mass initiation. The experience need not be expressed in occult terms and in the majority of cases will not be; the individual initiate who takes this initiation is aware of great changes in his attitude to himself, to his fellowmen, to circumstances and to his interpretation of life events. These are peculiarly the reactions which attend the first initiation; a new orientation to life and a new world of thought are registered by the initiate. This will be equally true on a large scale where modern man, the world initiate of the first degree, is concerned. Men will recognise the evidences in many lives of the emergence of the Christ-consciousness, and the standard of living will increasingly be adjusted to the truth as it exists in the teachings of the Christ.

This developing Christ-consciousness in the masses of men will create necessarily a ferment in the daily life of peoples everywhere; the life of the personality, oriented hitherto to the attaining of material and purely selfish ends, will be at war with the new and inner realisation; the "carnal" man (to use the words of Paul, the initiate) will be battling the spiritual man, each seeking to achieve control. In the early stages, after the "birth" and during the "infancy of the Christ-Child" (again speaking in symbols), the material aspect is triumphant. Later, the Christ life triumphs. This you well know. Each initiation indicates a stage in the growth and the development of this new factor in the human consciousness and expression, and this continues until the third initiation, when there emerges the "full-grown man in Christ". The initiate is then ready, at the fifth initiation, to register, realise and record the long awaited revelation.

In connection with the individual and the first initiation, the seventh ray is always active and the man is enabled consciously to register the fact of initiation because either the brain or the mind (and frequently both) are controlled by the seventh ray. It is this fact which is of importance today in connection with humanity, for it will enable mankind to pass through the door admitting them to the first initiatory process. It will be apparent to you why the present period in which human beings (in large groups) can take the first initiation corresponds to a situation in which bread is the major interest of men everywhere. Humanity will pass through this "birth" initiation and manifest the Christ life on a large scale for the first time during a period of economic adjustment of which the word "bread" is but a symbol. This period started in the year 1825 and will continue until the end of this century. The unfoldment of the Christ life—as a result of the presence and activities of the second divine aspect of love—will result in the ending of economic fear, and the "house of bread" will become the "house of plenty". Bread—as the symbol of material human need—will eventually be controlled by a vast group of initiates of the first initiation—by those whose lives are beginning to be controlled by the Christ-consciousness, which is the consciousness of responsibility and service. These initiates exist in their thousands today; they will be present in their millions by the time the year 2025 arrives. All this reorientation and unfoldment will be the result of the activity of the seventh ray and of the impact of its radiation upon humanity.

The seventh ray is, par excellence, the medium of relationship. It brings together the two fundamental aspects of spirit and matter. It relates soul and form and, where humanity is concerned, it relates soul and personality. In the first initiation, it makes the initiate aware of that relation; it enables him to take advantage of this "approaching duality" and—by the perfecting of the contact—to produce upon the physical plane the emergence into manifestation of the "new man". At the first initiation, through the stimulation brought about by seventh ray energy, the personality of the initiate and the hovering overshadowing soul are consciously brought together; the initiate then knows that he is—for the first time—a soul-infused personality. His task is now to grow into the likeness of what he essentially is. This development is demonstrated at the third initiation, that of the Transfiguration.

The major function of this seventh ray is to bring together the negative and positive aspects of the natural processes. It consequently governs the sex relationship of all forms; it is the potency underlying the marriage relation, and hence as this ray comes into manifestation in this world cycle, we have the appearance of fundamental sex problems—license, disturbance in the marriage relation, divorce and the setting in motion of those forces which will eventually produce a new attitude to sex and the establishing of those practices, attitudes and moral perceptions which will govern the relation between the sexes during the coming New Age.

The first initiation is therefore closely related to this problem. The seventh ray governs the sacral centre and the sublimation of its energy into the throat or into the higher creative centre; this ray is therefore setting in motion a period of tremendous creative activity, both on

The Seventh Ray and Initiation

the material plane through the stimulation of the sex life of all peoples and in the three worlds through the stimulation brought about when soul and form are consciously related. The first major proof that humanity (through the medium of the majority of its advanced people) has undergone the first initiation will be the appearance of a cycle of entirely new creative art. This creative urge will take forms which will express the new incoming energies. Just as the period governed by the sixth ray has culminated in a world wherein men work in great workshops and factories to produce the plethora of objects men deem needful for their happiness and well-being, so in the seventh ray cycle we shall see men engaged on an even larger scale in the field of creative art. Devotion to objects will eventually be superseded by the creation of that which will more truly express the Real; ugliness and materiality will give place to beauty and reality. On a large scale, humanity has already been "led from darkness to light" and the light of knowledge fills the land. In the period which lies ahead and under the influencing radiation of the seventh ray, humanity will be "led from the unreal to the Real". This the first initiation makes possible for the individual and will make possible for the mass of men.

Seventh ray energy is the energy needed to bring order out of chaos and rhythm to replace disorder. It is this energy which will bring in the new world order for which all men wait; it will restore the ancient landmarks, indicate the new institutions and forms of civilisation and culture which human progress demands, and nurture the new life and the new states of consciousness which advanced humanity will increasingly register. Nothing can arrest this activity; all that is happening today as men search for the new ways, for organised unity and peaceful security, is being implemented through the incoming Ray of Order or Ceremonial Magic. The white magic of right human relations cannot be stopped; it must inevitably demonstrate effectively, because the energy of this seventh ray is present, and the Lord of the Ray is cooperating with the Lord of the World to bring about the needed "re-forming". Soul-infused personalities, acting under this ray influence, will create the new world, express the new qualities and institute those new regimes and organised modes of creative activity which will demonstrate the new livingness and the new techniques of living. It is the distortion of these seventh ray ideals and the prostitution of this incoming energy to serve the unenlightened and selfish ambitions of greedy men which has produced those totalitarian systems which today so terribly imprison the free spirit of men.

To sum up what I have said:

1. The energy of the seventh ray is the potent agent of initiation when taken on the physical plane, that is, during the process of the first initiation.

2. Its effect upon humanity will be:

   a. To bring about the birth of the Christ-consciousness among the masses of intelligently aspiring human beings.

   b. To set in motion certain relatively new evolutionary processes which will transform humanity (the world disciple) into humanity (the world initiate).

   c. To establish in a new and intelligible manner the ever-existent sense of relationship and thus bring about upon the physical plane right human relations. The agent of this is goodwill, a reflection of the will-to-good of the first divine aspect. Of this first Ray of Will or Purpose, goodwill is the reflection.

   d. To readjust negative and positive relationships, and—today—this will be carried forward primarily in connection with the sex relation and marriage.

   e. To intensify human creativity and thus bring in the

The Seventh Ray and Initiation

new art as a basis for the new culture and as a conditioning factor in the new civilisation.

f. To reorganise world affairs and so initiate the new world order. This is definitely in the realm of ceremonial magic.

3. The stimulation of this seventh ray will, in relation to the individual initiate,

a. Bring into being upon the mental plane a widespread and recognised relation between the soul and the mind.

b. Produce a measure of order in the emotional processes of the initiate, thus aiding the preparatory work of the second initiation.

c. Enable the initiate—upon the physical plane—to establish certain service relationships, to learn the practice of elementary white magic, and to demonstrate the first stage of a truly creative life.

As far as the individual initiate is concerned, the effect of seventh ray energy in his life is potent in the extreme; this is easily realised, owing to the fact that his mind and his brain are conditioned by the seventh ray at the time that the initiatory process is consciously taking place. The effect of this upon the mental plane is similar to that seen—on a much larger scale—in the planet, for it was this ray energy which the planetary Logos utilised when He brought together the major dualities of spirit and matter at the commencement of His creative work. The two aspects of the mind (the lower concrete mind and the soul, the Son of Mind) become more closely related and enter eventually into a conscious recognised association *on the astral plane*; it is the seventh ray which restores order within the astral consciousness, and (on the mental plane) it is this influence which produces creativity, the organising of the life, and the bringing together "within the head" of the lower and higher energies in such a manner that "the Christ is born". This latter point we shall consider in some detail when we take up the significance of the initiations; we shall then find that the relationship between the pituitary body and the pineal gland is involved.

Finally, it is seventh ray energy which—in the initiatory process between the first and second initiations—enables the initiate (in his physical plane life) to demonstrate a developing sense of order and of organisation, to express consciously and increasingly a desire to help his fellowmen, and thereby establish relationship with them, and to make his life creative in many ways.

All these factors are embryonic in his nature, but he now begins to *consciously* lay the foundation for the future initiatory work; the physical disciplines are at this time of great importance, though their value is frequently overemphasised and their effect is not always good; the relationships established and fostered are sometimes of small value, owing to the disciple being usually self-centred and thus lacking—from ignorance and lack of discrimination—complete purity of motive. Nevertheless, the changes brought about by the influence of this ray become increasingly effective from life to life; the disciple's relation to the Hierarchy, the reorganising of his life on the physical plane, and his growing effort to demonstrate the esoteric sense of white magic will become more and more vital, until he is ready for the second initiation.

RI 567-75

The third and fifth rays are peculiarly active upon the Path of Discipleship, just as the sixth and fourth are dominant upon the Path of Evolution and the first and seventh upon the Path of Initiation. The second ray controls and dominates all the other rays, as you well know.

EA 165

The Seventh Ray and Initiation

Thus the work of magical reformation starts, and it is here that the influence of the seventh ray (which governs the first initiation) enters in; one of the functions of this ray is to bring together soul and body, the higher and the lower, life and form, spirit and matter. This is the creative task confronting the disciple who is engaged in lifting the energies of the sacral centre to the throat centre and of establishing a right relation between the personality and the soul. Just as the antahkarana has to be constructed and established as a bridge of light between the Spiritual Triad and the soul-infused personality, so a similar bridge or correspondence is established between the soul and the personality, and, in connection with the mechanism of the disciple, between the two head centres and the two glands within the head.

When that line of light has related the higher spiritual aspects and the lower, and when the sacral centre and the throat centre are in true related alignment, the initiate-disciple becomes a creative worker under the divine Plan and a "magical exponent" of the divine building work; he is then a constructive force, wielding energy consciously on the physical plane. He creates forms as expressions of reality. This is the true work of magic.

You can see, therefore, that in the creative work three energies are brought into a related activity:

1. The energy concentrated in the ajna centre and which is indicative of the personality life.

2. The energy concentrated in the head centre as a result of soul activity.

3. The energy of the seventh Ray of Ceremonial Order or Magic, making possible true creative activity under the divine Plan.

There is nothing spectacular to be told anent the first initiation; the initiate-disciple still works in the dimly lit "cave of the spiritual birth"; he has to continue his struggle to reveal divinity, primarily on the physical plane—symbolised for us in the word "Bethlehem" which means the "house of bread"; he has to learn the dual function of "lifting up the lower energies into the light" and—at the same time—of "bringing down the higher energies into bodily expression". Thus he becomes a white magician.

At this initiation he sees, for the first time, what are the major energies which he must bring into expression, and this vision is summed up for him in the *Old Commentary* in the following words:

"When the Rod of Initiation descends and touches the lower part of the spine, there is a lifting up; where the eyes are opened in the light, that which must be lowered into form is now perceived. The vision is acknowledged. The burden of the future is assumed. The cave is lighted up and the new man issues forth."

RI 672-73

CHAPTER TEN

EFFECTS OF THE INCOMING SEVENTH RAY

Masonry

Under this seventh ray influence the Masonic Fraternity will come into a new and pronounced spiritual activity and begin to approximate its true function and to fulfill its long-seen destiny. One point it might be of interest here to note. During the period of activity of the sixth ray the Fraternity fell into a crystallised and sectarian attitude, along with the many other grouped circles. It fell also into the snare of materialism, and the outer form has for centuries been of more importance in the eyes of Masons than the inner spiritual meaning. The symbols and the system of allegories have been emphasized, whilst that which they were intended to convey and to reveal to the initiated has been quite forgotten. Also, the trend of the attention of a lodge of Masons, and the main emphasis, has been potently placed on the function and place of the W.M., and not upon the inner significance of the work upon the floor of the Temple. The lodge has not been regarded as an integrated functioning entity. This must and will be changed, and the potency and the effectiveness of the lodge work and ceremonial will be demonstrated. It will be seen that in the regularity of the rituals and the sanctified formality of the ordained ceremonials lies the true meaning of the work and the use of the *Word*. The coming era of group work and power and of organised synthetic ritualistic activity will profoundly affect Masonry, as the importance of a central dominating figure passes out with the sixth ray influence and the true spiritual work and function of the lodge itself is understood.

EPI 368-69

The seventh Ray of Ceremonial Order or Magic embodies a curious quality which is the outstanding characteristic of the particular Life which ensouls this ray. It is the quality or principle which is the coordinating factor unifying the inner quality and the outer tangible form or appearance. This work goes on primarily on etheric levels and involves physical energy. This is the true magical work. I should like to point out that when the fourth ray and the seventh ray come into incarnation together, we shall have a most peculiar period of revelation and of light-bringing. It is said of this time that then "the temple of the Lord will take on an added glory and the Builders will rejoice together." This will be the high moment of the Masonic work, spiritually understood. The Lost Word will then be recovered and uttered for all to hear, and the Master will arise and walk among His builders in the full light of the glory which shines from the east.

The spiritualising of forms might be regarded as the main work of the seventh ray, and it is this principle of fusion, of coordination and of blending which is active on etheric levels every time a soul comes into incarnation and a child is born on earth.

EPI 52-53

...Masonry—being on the first ray and emanating, consequently, from Shamballa—aids the process of visualisation. It gives colour and performance of a tangible kind to inner, subjective activity. Visualisation is a powerful agent in the evocation of the creative imagination. Let me here give you a hint. If you use this idea in the planning of the work which you seek to do for the Hierarchy and for which we are seeking to hold you responsible, and if you carry into all that work the ideal of ritual, of rhythm and of energy distribution, you will evoke a synthetic pattern, a unified procedure and a harmonious working out of the Plan.

DINAI 171-72

The Mysteries will restore colour and music as they essentially are to the world and do it in such a manner that the creative art of today will be to this new creative art what a child's building of wooden blocks is to a great cathedral such as Durham or Milan. The Mysteries, when restored, will make real—in a sense incomprehensible to you at present—the nature of religion, the purpose of science and the goal of education. These are not what you think today.

The ground is being prepared at this time for this great restoration. The Churches and Masonry are today before the judgment seat of humanity's critical mind and the word has gone forth from that mass mind that both of them failed in their divinely assigned tasks. It is realised everywhere that new life must be poured in and great changes wrought in the awareness and in the training of those who work through and in these two media of truth. Those changes have not yet been carried out, for it will take a new vision and a new approach to life experience, and this only the coming generation is capable of giving; they and they alone can bring about the needed alterations and the revitalisation, but it can and will be done:

"That which is a mystery shall no longer be so, and that which has been veiled will now be revealed; that which has been withdrawn will emerge into the light, and all men shall see and together they shall rejoice. That time will come when desolation has wrought its beneficent work, when all things have been destroyed, and men, through suffering, have sought to be impressed by that which they had discarded in vain pursuit of that which was near at hand and easy of attainment. Possessed, it proved to be an agency of death—yet men sought life, not death."

So runs the *Old Commentary* when referring to the present cycle through which mankind is passing.

RI 332

The Mineral Kingdom

The Ray of Ceremonial Order has special significance at this time; it controls life in the mineral world, and in the final stages of involutionary life at the point where the upward turn of evolution is made. Through Ceremonial Order comes the control of the lesser builders, the elemental forces, the point of synthesis in the lowest plane of all, the period of transition. In all such periods the seventh ray comes in (as now) the Ray of Law and Order, of accurate arrangement and formation. It is the reflection on the physical plane of the Power and Activity Aspects working in synthesis. Rays 1,3,7, have an interplay, as we know. Ray seven is the appearance in combination of the forces of evolution. It is the manifestation of Power and Activity on the lowest plane of all. It is allied to the laws of the third and seventh planes, Disintegration and Death, for all periods of transition are periods of the destruction and building of forms, and the shattering of the old in order that newer and better chalices of life may be constructed.

CF 589

The influence of the organising seventh ray is best seen in the amazing and geometrically perfect structure of the elements, as revealed by the microscope and by a study of the atom. As this treatise is intended for the reader who has no academic or scientific training, it will suffice to say that the mineral kingdom is a result of the "ritual of rhythm", as are all the basic forms upon which the myriad of structures in manifestation are constructed and founded. The system of numbers demonstrates in its fullest beauty in this kingdom, and there is no form and no numerological relation which cannot be discovered in minute form in this foundational kingdom, under the occult microscopic vision. Two factors determine the structures found in the mineral kingdom:

1. The seventh great impulse, or the will to organise.

2. The urge to create, or the initial rhythm which led the solar Logos to take form.

The work of the seventh Lord and of the first Lord is essentially the work of the architect and of the magician, and Their efforts are seen to perfection in the mineral world. This will not, however, be realised in full potency and magical revelation until the inner eye of true vision is developed and the forms underlying the creative work in the other kingdoms in nature are seen in their real values....

I. The Mineral Kingdom

Influence	The seventh ray of organisation and the first ray of power are the dominant factors.
Results	The evolutionary results are radiation and potency, a static potency, underlying the rest of the natural scheme.
Process	Condensation.
Secret	Transmutation. *The Treatise on Cosmic Fire* defines this as follows: "Transmutation is the passage across from one state of being to another through the agency of fire."
Purpose	To demonstrate the radio-activity of life.
Divisions	Base metals, standard metals, precious stones.
Objective agency	Fire. Fire is the initiating factor in this kingdom.
Subjective agency	Sound.
Quality	Extreme density. Inertia. Brilliance.

Students must remember that we are not dealing with the elements and atoms, as we study this kingdom. They are the substance out of which all the mineral forms are made. But we are dealing with the mineral forms as they manifest in the concrete world. We are considering the tangible and objective world. The internal constitution and geometrical formation of the minerals do not come under our subject matter. This is not a scientific treatise, as usually understood, but a study in quality and consciousness as they affect the form aspect. Much, if not nearly all that exoteric science has posited regarding the mineral kingdom can, for ordinary uses, be accepted as relative fact. But two points should be considered, and they are:

1. The consciousness aspect of the mineral world.
2. The transmutation of forms by fire in that kingdom, leading to an ultimate radiation.

The best known example of the effect of the initiation of the mineral by fire can be seen in the great transition and transformation, allotropically brought about, from the carbon stage to that of the perfect diamond. A further qualitative stage can be seen as the radiation or the throwing off of rays, as in radium.

That there are three stages in the evolutionary processes in the mineral kingdom must be borne in mind, and these (though apparently unrelated to each other from the angle of modern science) are nevertheless subjectively and essentially part of a tremendous inner process. These stages are the correspondences in the mineral kingdom to the stages of animal consciousness, of self-consciousness, and of the radiant group consciousness of the soul. There is a fourth stage of potency or of organised expressed power, but this lies ahead, and is the analogy in this kingdom to the life of the Monad, as expressed in the solar consciousness of the initiates of high degree.

Just as science has discovered the ninety-two elements so that the list of the possible elements is relatively complete, so eventually science will have arranged the progressive tables which will show the three stages of the life cycle of every mineral leading from the static mineral stage, such as carbon, through that of the crystal, semi-precious stone and precious stone to that of the radio-active substance. In the determining of this development it is impossible for man as yet to see the relations, for the cycles covered are so vast, the action of the fire in these tremendous periods so varying, and the recognition of the intermediate stages so difficult, that aught that I could say would but feed amusement and incredulity. But two basic premises can be laid down:

1. That the many mineral substances fall naturally into seven main groups, corresponding to the seven subdivisions of the influencing rays, those of organisation and power.
2. That only in those world cycles when the seventh ray is in manifestation, and therefore supremely powerful, do certain hidden changes take place in these seven groups. These are the correspondences, in the mineral evolution, to the seven initiations of man.

At these times there is an increased radiatory activity. This can be noted at this time in the discovery of radio-active substance, as the incoming ray increases its potency, decade by decade. A certain amount of radiation is basic and fundamental in any world cycle. But when the seventh ray comes in there is an intensification of that radiation, and new substances appear to come into new activity. This intensification leaves the entire mineral kingdom, as a whole, more radio-active than before, until this increased radiation becomes in its turn basic and fundamental. As the seventh ray passes cyclically out of manifestation a certain measure of inertia settles down on the kingdom, though that which is radiatory continues its activity. In this way the radiation of the mineral world steadily increases as the cycles come and go, and there is necessarily a paralleling effect upon the higher three kingdoms. People today have no idea what effect this radiation (due to the incoming ray) will have, not only upon the surrounding mineral world but on the vegetable kingdom (which has its roots in the mineral kingdom), and upon men and animals in lesser degree. The power of the incoming cosmic rays has called forth the more easily recognised radio-activity with which modern science is now concerned. It was three seventh ray disciples who "interpreted" these rays to man. I refer to the Curies and to Millikan. Being themselves on the seventh ray, they had the necessary psychic equipment and responsiveness to enable them intuitively to recognise their own ray vibration in the mineral kingdom.

The seventh ray is one of organised ritual, and in form building this quality is basic and necessary. The processes found in the mineral kingdom are profoundly geometrical. The first ray is that of dynamic will or power, and—speaking symbolically—when perfected forms and organised vehicles and dynamic power are related and unified, then we shall have a full expression, at the point of deepest and densest concretion, of the mind of God in form, with a radiation which will be dynamically effective.

Again speaking symbolically (and what else is possible when dealing with a mechanism as yet so inadequate as the mind and brain of the average aspirant?), the mineral kingdom marks the point of unique condensation. This is produced under the action of fire and by the pressure of the "divine idea". Esoterically speaking, we have, in the mineral world, the divine Plan hidden in the geometry of a crystal, and God's radiant beauty stored in the colour of a precious stone. In miniature and at the lowest point of manifestation, we find the divine concepts working out. The goal of the universal concept is seen when the jewel rays forth its beauty, and when radium sends forth its rays, both destructive and constructive. If you could really understand the history of a crystal, you would enter into the glory of God. If you could enter into the attractive and the repulsive consciousness of a piece of iron or lead, you would see revealed the complete story of evolution. If you could study the hidden processes which go on under the influence of fire, you would enter into the secret of initiation. When the day comes when the history of the mineral kingdom can be grasped by the illumined seer, he will then see the long road that the diamond has travelled, and—by analogy—the long road that all sons of God traverse, governed by the same laws and unfolding the same consciousness.

The seventh ray, when manifesting on the seventh plane, (as is now the case), is peculiarly potent, and its effect upon the mineral kingdom is consequently dynamically felt. If it is true that there is only one substance and one spirit, that "matter is spirit at the lowest point of its cyclic activity" and spirit is matter at its highest, then the ray of ceremonial order or ritual is but an expression of its polar opposite—the first ray of will or power. It is the expression of the same potency under another aspect. This means therefore that:

1. The power or will of God expresses itself through the organised systematised processes of the seventh ray. The geometrical faculty of the Universal Mind finds its most material perfection on the physical or seventh plane, working through the seventh ray. So the mineral kingdom came into being as this major expression. It holds in solution all the forces and those chemicals and minerals which are needed by the forms in the other material kingdoms.

2. The mineral kingdom is therefore the most concrete expression of the dual unity of power and order. It constitutes the "foundation" of the ordered physical

structure or the universe of our planet.
3. The rhythmic ritualistic adaptability of the seventh ray, plus the dynamic will of the power ray, are needed in conjunction for the full working out of the Plan, as it is found in the mind of God.

This is why, in this present period of transition, the Lord of the seventh ray is taking over the control of affairs and the ordered working out of the Plan, so as eventually to restore stability to the planet and give the incoming Aquarian influences a stable and extended field in which to work. This we shall later elaborate when we take up the study of the zodiacal signs and their relation to the rays.

We shall now touch upon the next two points—condensation and its hidden secret, transmutation. From the standpoint of external matter, the mineral kingdom marks the point of densest expression of the life of God in substance, and its outstanding, though oft unrealised, characteristic is imprisoned or unexpressed power. Speaking in symbols, a volcano in eruption is a mild expression of this power. From the standpoint of esoteric substance, the four ethers are far more dense and "substantial". This modern science has also told us, positing the hypothetical ether. This fifth kingdom (counting occultly from the egoic kingdom downwards) is a reflection of these four ethers, and the point of their densest concretion. Just as they "sub-stand" or form the basis of the manifested world, and are regarded as the "true form", so the mineral kingdom is the fundamental kingdom in the three worlds, under the Law of Correspondences. It is, in a most peculiar sense, "precipitated etheric substance", and is a condensation or externalisation of the etheric planes. This solidification or precipitation—resulting in the production of dense objective or solid matter—is the tangible result of the interplay of the energies and qualities of the first and seventh rays. Their united will and ordered rhythm have produced this

Earth and the molten content of the planet, regarding the earth as the crust.

In the turning of the great wheel, cycle after cycle, these two rays come into functioning activity, and in between their objective cycles the other rays dominate and participate in the great work. The result of this interplay of psychic potencies will manifest in the eventual transmutation of the earth substance, and its resolution back again into that of which is it the objective condensation. Again language fails to find the needed terms. They are as yet nonexistent. I mention this as an indication of the difficulty of our subject. Intangible etheric substance has been condensed into the dense tangible objective world. This—under the evolutionary plan—has to be again transmuted into its original condition, plus the gain of ordered rhythm and the tendencies and qualities wrought into the consciousness of its atoms and elements through the experience of externalisation. This resolution is noted by us as radiation and the radio-active substances. We are looking on at the transmutation process. The resolving agencies are fire, intense heat and pressure. These three agencies have already succeeded in bringing about the divisions of the mineral kingdom into three parts: the baser metals, as they are called, the standard metals (such as silver and gold and platinum), and the semi-precious stones and crystals. The precious jewels are a synthesis of all three—one of the basic syntheses of evolution. In this connection, some correspondences between the mineral kingdom and the human evolutionary cycles might here be noted:

1. The base metals . . . . physical plane. Dense Consciousness.
   The first initiation.

2. The standard metals . . . . . . astral plane. Self-consciousness.
   The second initiation.

3. The semi-precious stones . . . . . . mental plane. Radiant consciousness.

> The third initiation.

4. The precious jewels . . . . egoic consciousness and achievement.

> The fourth initiation.

The correspondences of fire, heat and pressure in the evolution of the human being are self-evident, and their work can be seen paralleling that in the mineral kingdom.

The mineral kingdom is governed astrologically by Taurus, and there is a symbolic relation between the "eye" in the head of the Bull, the third eye, the light in the head, and the diamond. The consciousness of the Buddha has been called the "diamond-eye".

EPI 221-30

Animals

The Incoming Seventh Ray and the Animal Kingdom

1. The animal kingdom is to the human body what the dense physical body is to the seven principles.
2. The animal kingdom is the mother aspect, prior to the over-shadowing of the Holy Ghost.
3. The animal kingdom is the field of individualisation.
4. Since Atlantean days the animal kingdom has been occupied with the development of karma.
5. Domestic animals constitute the heart centre in the life of the Entity Who ensouls the animal kingdom.
6. The animal kingdom does not react strongly to the 7th ray.
7. The human kingdom does, but the 7th ray will have three effects in relation to the two kingdoms and their interplay:
   a. It will refine the animal bodies.
   b. It will bring about a closer relation between men and animals.

> c. It will cause a great destruction of the present animal forms.
>
> EPI 415

...the seventh ray influence will have three definite effects upon the fourth and third kingdoms in nature. These are as follows:

1. All animal bodies will be steadily refined and in the case of humanity consciously refined, and so brought to a higher and more specialised state of development. This is today proceeding with rapidity. Diet and athletics, open air and sunshine are doing much for the race and in the next two generations fine bodies and sensitive natures will make their appearance and the soul will have far better instruments through which to work.

2. The relation between the human and the animal kingdoms will become increasingly close. The service of the animal to man is well recognised and of ceaseless expression. The service of man to the animals is not yet understood though some steps in the right direction are being taken. There must eventually be a close synthesis and sympathetic coordination between them and when this is the case some very extraordinary occurrences of animal mediumship under human inspiration will take place. By means of this, the intelligent factor in the animal (of which instinct is the embryonic manifestation) will be rapidly developed and this is one of the outstanding results of the intended human-animal relationship.

3. There will be, as a consequence of this quickened evolution, the rapid destruction of certain types of animal bodies. Very low grade human bodies will disappear, causing a general shift in the racial types towards a higher standard. Many species of animals will also die out and are today disappearing, and hence the increas-

ing emphasis upon the preservation of animals and the establishing of game preserves.

DN 124-25

Much of profound interest is on its way as a result of this seventh ray activity. For one thing, though the animal kingdom reacts but little to this type of influence, yet there are going to be very definite results within the soul of the animal form. The door of individualisation or of entrance into the human kingdom has been closed since Atlantean times, but under the new influence it will be partially opened; it will be set ajar, so that a few animals will respond to soul stimulation and discover that their rightful place is on the human side of the dividing door. Part of the reorganisation which will go on as a result of the seventh ray activity will concern the relation of humanity to the animal kingdom and the establishing of better and of closer relations. This will lead men to take advantage of another effect of the seventh ray, which is its power to refine the matter out of which the forms are built. The animal body of man has received much scientific attention during the past one hundred years, and medicine and surgery have reached great heights of achievement. The framework of man, his body, and its internal systems (with their diverse rituals) are now understood as never before, and this has been the result of the incoming ray force with its power to apply knowledge to the magical work. When this knowledge is applied intensively to the animal world much new and interesting data will be discovered; when the differences between the physical bodies of the animals and those of humanity have been more closely investigated there will appear a new and very fruitful field of study. These differences are largely in the realm of the nervous systems; not enough attention has been paid for instance to the fact that the brain of the animal is really in the region of the solar plexus, whilst the human brain, the controlling agent, is in the head, and works through the medium of the spinal column. When scientists know exactly why the animal does not use the brain in the head as does man, they will arrive at a fuller knowledge of the law governing cycles.

EPI 371-72

b. A*nimals and human beings and the rays.* We will now take up two points and study the effect of the incoming force on the human and animal kingdoms.

These points are of profound interest to the occult student for two reasons. The topic we have now to consider is the effect of the incoming seventh ray during the coming centuries upon the animal kingdom and the deva evolution. The profundity of the interest lies in the fact that in the one case we are dealing with the evolution immediately behind the human and from which man is not as yet wholly emancipated, and in the other we are concerning ourselves with a paralleling evolution, and one that is of vast importance in the scheme of things. Let us take up first this *seventh ray and its effect upon the animal kingdom....*

...The effect upon the animal kingdom of the force of this ray will be far less than upon the human, for it is not yet ready to respond to the vibration of this planetary Logos, and will not be until the sixth round when His influence will bring about great events. Nevertheless, certain effects might here be noticed.

Owing to the increased activity of the deva evolution, and specially of the devas of the ethers, the lesser builders will be stimulated to build, with greater facility, bodies of a more responsive nature, and the etheric bodies of both men and animals and also their responsiveness to force or prana will be more adequate. During the sixth subrace, disease as we know it in both kingdoms will be materially lessened owing to the pranic response of the etheric bodies. This will likewise bring about changes in the dense physical body and the bodies of both men and animals will be smaller, more refined, more finely attuned to vibration, and consequently more fitted to express essential purpose.

Owing to the recognition by man of the value of mantrams, and his gradual comprehension of the true ceremonial of evolution, coupled with the use of sound and colour, the animal kingdom will be better understood, and better trained, considered and utilised. Indications of this already can be seen; for instance, in all our current magazines at this time, stories which deal with the psychology of animals, and with their mental attitude to man, are constantly appearing, and by the means of these and through the force of the incoming ray, man may (if he cares to do so) come to a much wider sympathy with his brothers of less degree. Thus by the turning by man of his thought force upon the animals, stimulation of their latent mentality will ensue, leading in due course of time to the crisis in the next round. More attention should be paid by occult students to the effect of the consciousness of one group upon another group, and the advancement of the lesser, by the means of the stimulating power of the greater, should be studied....

CF 457-63

Devas

Our subject for immediate consideration concerns the *deva evolution,* and the effect of the incoming ray upon them.

The first point to be noted is that this influence at this time affects primarily the devas of the physical plane, the devas of the ethers, or of the shadows, as they are sometimes called, and not, to the same extent, the devas of the astral or mental planes. Every ray affects in more or less degree the plane or subplane which is its numerical corre-

Effects of the Incoming Seventh Ray 173

spondence; the student should bear this in mind, and should therefore recollect that for all purposes of investigation at this time the seventh Ray of Ceremonial Magic will have a powerful influence:

On the seventh or physical plane, regarding it as a unit.

On the seventh subplane or the lowest subplane on the physical, the astral and the mental planes.

On the seventh or lowest human principle: prana in the etheric body.

On all Monads in incarnation who are seventh ray Monads.

On a peculiar group of devas who are the agents, or "mediates" between magicians (either white or black) and the elemental forces. This group is occultly known as "The Mediatory Seventh", and is divided into 2 divisions:

a. Those working with evolutionary forces.

b. Those working with involutionary forces.

One group is the agent of constructive purpose, and the other of destructive. More need not be submitted anent this group as they are not easily contacted, fortunately for man, and can as yet only be reached by a particular group ritual *accurately* performed—a thing as yet practically unknown. The Masons eventually will be one of the chief agents of contact, and as men are as yet not ready for such power as this will put into their hands, true masonry will develop but slowly. Nevertheless, under the magnetic force of this seventh ray, the growth of masonry is inevitably sure.

This Ray of Ceremonial Magic will consequently have a very profound effect upon the physical plane, for not only is this plane coming under its cyclic force but at all times its planetary Logos has a special effect upon it; the Raja-Lord of this plane is what is occultly termed the "Reflection in the Water of Chaos" of the planetary Logos. Hence in the matter of this plane (which is the body of the

Raja-Lord) certain very definite events are occurring which—though invisible to the ordinary man—are apparent to the eye of the spiritual man or adept.

The matter of the plane becomes receptive to positive force for the feminine or deva aspect, being negative, becomes responsive to the positive energy of the Heavenly Man. This energy, finding the line of least resistance, pours into the substance of the plane, or the substantial body of the Deva Lords. Owing to the receptive condition of this body it follows certain lines and produces definitely *constructive* results.

Constructive results transpire in the negative etheric matter of the plane and on the four higher subplanes. On the lower three a contrary effect is produced, and the energy of the Heavenly Man will lead to the destruction of form, preparatory to the building work. The building ever originates on, and proceeds from, etheric levels. Cataclysms of a world wide nature will occur during the next one thousand years; continents will be shaken; lands will be raised and submerged, culminating in the profound material disaster which will overtake the world towards the close of the fourth branch race of the sixth subrace. This will usher in the infant sixth root race.

The devas of the ethers, with which we are most concerned, will be affected in several ways, and the results upon the other evolutions will be far-reaching. We must remember always that the devas are the qualities and attributes of matter, the active builders, who work consciously or unconsciously upon the plane. Here I would point out that all the devas of the higher levels of the mental plane, for instance, and of the systemic planes from there on to the centre (the divine plane, the plane of the Logos, sometimes called Adi) cooperate consciously, and are of high rank in the system, and of position equal to all the ranks and grades of the Hierarchy from a first degree initiate up

Effects of the Incoming Seventh Ray 175

to, but not including, the Lord of the World Himself. Below these higher levels, where the concrete is touched, we have lesser grades of devas who work unconsciously, with the following exceptions, who are conscious forces and entities and of high position:

a. The Raja-lord of a plane.
b. Seven devas who work under Him, and are the entities who inform the matter of the seven sub-planes.
c. Fourteen representatives of the rays, Who cycle into and out of power, according to the ray, waxing or waning.
d. Four devas who are the plane representatives of the four Maharajas (the Lords of Karma) and are the focal points for karmic influence in connection with man. The four Maharajas are the dispensers of karma to the Heavenly Men, and thus to the cells, centres, and organs of His body necessarily; but the whole system works through graded representatives; the same laws govern these agents of plane karma as govern the systemic and cosmic, and during plane manifestation they are, for instance, the only unit *in form* permitted to pass beyond the plane ring-pass-not. All other units in manifestation on a plane have to discard the vehicle through which they function before they can pass on to subtler levels....

The deva evolution will, through this seventh ray force have much to do with the transmission of prana to units of the three higher kingdoms of nature, and this easier transmission (from the etheric levels of the physical plane) will parallel a correspondingly easier transmission of spiritual or psychical force from the fourth cosmic ether, the buddhic plane. The results of this pranic transmission will be more healthy physical bodies among the sons of men. This need not be looked for at this time, and will only begin to be noticeable about three hundred years hence, when the incoming seventh ray Egos will be numerically strong enough to be recognised as the prevailing type for a certain period. Their physical bodies, owing to their being built for seventh ray force will respond more readily than the others, though first ray Egos and fifth ray Egos will benefit enormously from this influence. The etheric devas will build during a peculiarly favourable period, and the physical bodies then constructed will be distinguished by:

a. Resilience,
b. Enormous physical magnetism,
c. Ability to reject false magnetism,
d. Capacity to absorb solar rays,
e. Great strength and resistance,
f. A delicacy and refinement in appearance as yet unknown.

The etheric levels of the plane will be full of an increased activity, and slowly but surely, as the decades slip away, man will become conscious of these levels, and aware of their inhabitants. The immediate effect of this greater etheric energy will be that a numerically larger number of people will possess etheric vision, and will be able normally and naturally to live consciously on etheric levels. The majority of men only function consciously on the three lower levels of the physical—the gaseous, the liquid, and the dense—and the etheric levels are as sealed to them as are the astral. In the coming centuries, man's normal habitat will be the entire physical plane up to, though not including, the second subplane. The fourth and third etheric levels will be as familiar to him as the usual physical landscape to which he is now accustomed.

The centre of attention of medical and scientific students will be focussed on the etheric body, and the dependence of the physical body upon the etheric body will be recognised. This will change the attitude of the medical profession, and magnetic healing and vibratory stimulation will supersede the present methods of surgery and drug assimilation. Man's vision being then normally etheric, will have the effect of forcing him to recognise that which is now called the "unseen world", or the superphysical. Men in their etheric bodies will be noted, and communicated with, and the devas and elementals of the ethers will be studied and recognised. When this is so, then the true use of ceremonial ritual as a protection and safeguard to man will assume its right place.

The work of the devas in connection with the animal and the vegetable kingdoms will be likewise recognised, and much that is now possible through ignorance will become impossible and obsolete. The time will come, when the attitude of man to the animal kingdom will be revolutionised, and the slaughter, ill-treatment, and that form of cruelty called "sport", will be done away with.

A mysterious change in the attitude of men and women to the sex question, marriage and the work of procreation will result from the development of etheric vision, and the consequent recognition of the devas. This change will be based on the realisation of the true nature of matter, or of the mother aspect, and of the effect of the Sun upon substance. The unity of life will be a known and scientific fact, and *life in matter* will no longer be a theory but a fundamental of science. This cannot be enlarged upon here.

CF 465-75

The fifth principle of manas is at this time beginning to demonstrate mainly through the seventh type of force (or the fifth when considering only the Brahma aspect of manifestation). It will be immediately apparent, therefore, that this incoming ray is peculiarly situated at this time, and that its influence will be manifested under very favorable conditions. It is pouring its force out upon the seventh plane, the physical, during the fifth rootrace and the fifth subrace, and consequently the opportunity is great. In all that has been said anent the rays it will be apparent that from the present standpoint two are paramountly concerned with the evolution of man: the *fourth Ray of Harmony*, which is the dominant ray of the greater cycle which includes the fourth round and globe, and the *seventh Ray of Ceremonial Magic*, which is one of the foremost influences concerned in all objective manifestations. These two rays, or the force of these two planetary Logoi, are largely instrumental in bringing about coherency in our chain, the fourth of the fourth scheme, and on our physical globe, the Earth. The fourth and the seventh interact, one acting temporarily as a negative force and the other as a positive.

The fifth Kumara, the Lord of the seventh Ray (for it is necessary to keep in mind His dual position as one of the points of the five-pointed Star of Brahma, and as one of the Triangles in the seven-fold logoic body) has a unique position as the "Ruler of the Building Devas" of the physical plane, the devas of the ethers, in cooperation with their Deva Lord. He guides and directs the production of the form by means of certain occult words. He works, therefore, through the etheric body of all forms and it is through His inflowing force that we may look for that increased stimulation of the matter of the etheric brain which will make the physical brain receptive to the higher revealing truth, and will put into the hands of scientists the secrets of the fourth and third ethers. The development of the matter of the brain parallels the stage of development of its atomic correspondence, and in the vitalisation of the fifth spirilla and the consequent reflex action of the seventh, we may look to see the mind of man assume proportions, and attain achievement, as yet unthought and undreamt.

CF 440-41

...With the coming in of this seventh Ray of Ceremonial Magic, a tentative approximation of the two evolving groups [humanity and the deva kingdom—*Editors*] is to be somewhat permitted, though not as yet with the involving group. Remember this statement. The deva and human evolution will, during the next five hundred years, become somewhat more conscious of each other, and be able therefore more freely to co-operate. With this growing consciousness will be found a seeking after methods of communication. When the need of communication for constructive ends is sincerely felt, then, under the judicious guidance of the Masters, will certain of the old mantrams be permitted circulation. Their action, interaction and reaction will be closely studied and watched. It is hoped that the benefit to both groups will be mutual. The human evolution should give strength to the deva, and the deva, joy to the human. Man should communicate to the devas the objective point of view, while they in turn will pour in on him their healing magnetism. They are the custodians of prana, magnetism and vitality, just as man is the custodian of the fifth principle, or manas. I have given several hints here and more is not possible.

LOM 182-83

There is also a group of devas connected with the Lodge of Masters, whose work it is to build the aspirational forms towards which average man may aspire. They are divided into certain groups—three in number—connected with science, religion and philosophy, and through these groups of deva substance the Heads of the three departments reach men. It is one of Their channels for work. The Master Jesus is particularly active at this time along this line, working in collaboration with certain adepts on the scientific line, who—through the desired union of science and religion—seek to shatter the materialism of the west on the one hand and on the other the sentimental devotion of the many devotees of all faiths. This is made possible now through the passing out of the sixth ray and the coming in of the seventh.

CF 677-78

We will consider now the etheric levels of the physical plane or the four highest subplanes of the physical plane. These etheric levels are but gradations of physical plane matter of a rarer and more refined kind, but physical nevertheless. They are termed in most textbooks:

1. The first ether, or atomic matter.
2. The second ether, or sub-atomic matter.
3. The third ether, or super-etheric matter,
4. The fourth ether, or simply etheric matter.

The fourth ether is the only one as yet recognised by scientists, and is the subject of their present investigations, little though they may realise it.

On the atomic subplane are the permanent physical atoms of all humanity and the *appropriated atoms* of the deva kingdom. The devas do not develop as do the human race. They reincarnate in groups, and not as individuals, though each group is composed of units, and has nothing of the nature of the involutionary group soul. The group soul on the involutionary path and that upon the evolutionary are unlike; one is passing on to differentiation and is composed of entities animated by one general life; the other has differentiated, and each entity is a separate unit of the one life, complete in itself, yet one with the whole.

There are many types of life to be contacted on the four etheric levels, but we can only concern ourselves at present with the deva life, remembering that the deva evolution is of equal importance to that of the human. These devas are many in number, are of involutionary and evolutionary nature, and of all grades and types. Ruling over them on the physical plane is the great deva Kshiti. He is a deva of rank and power equal to a Chohan of a ray; He presides over everything outside the human kingdom upon the physical plane, and He has for His council the four subordinate deva lords of the four etheric levels. He, with these subordinate devas, presides over a subsidiary council of seven devas who handle all that concerns the deva evolution, and the work of the greater and the lesser builders.

The deva Ruler of the fourth, or lowest ether, has delegated a member of His council to meet with certain of the Masters at this time for two specific purposes, first, to see whether the approximation of the two lines of evolution, human and deva, might be now tentatively permitted, and, secondly, to reveal some of the methods of healing and the causes of physical disability which are inherent in the etheric double.

Devas of all kinds and colours are found on the physical etheric levels, but the prevailing hue is violet, hence the term so often employed, the "devas of the shadows". With the coming in of the ceremonial ray of violet, we have the amplification therefore of the violet vibration, always inherent on these levels, and the great opportunity therefore for contact between the two kingdoms. It is in the development of etheric vision (which is a capacity of the physical human eye) and not in clairvoyance that this mutual apprehension will become possible. With the coming in likewise of this ray will arrive those who belong thereon, with a natural gift of seeing etherically. Children will frequently be born who will see etherically as easily as the average human being sees physically; as conditions of harmony gradually evolve out of the present world chaos, devas and human beings will meet as friends.

As the two planes, astral and physical, merge and blend, and continuity of consciousness is experienced upon the two, it will be difficult for human beings to differentiate at first between devas of the astral plane, and those of the physical. At the beginning of this period of recognition, men will principally contact the violet devas, for those of the higher ranks amongst them are definitely making the attempt to contact the human. These devas of the shadows are of a dark purple on the fourth etheric level, of a lighter purple, much the same colour as violet, on the third etheric level, a light violet on the second, whilst on the atomic subplane they are of a glorious translucent lavender.

Some of the groups of devas to be contacted on the physical plane are as follows:

Four groups of violet devas, associated with the etheric doubles of all that exists on the physical plane. These four are in two divisions, those associated with the building of the etheric doubles, and those out of whose substance these doubles are built.

The green devas of the vegetable kingdom. These exist in two divisions also. They are of high development, and will be contacted principally along the lines of magnetisation. The greater devas of this order preside over the magnetic spots of the earth, guard the solitude of the forests, reserve intact spaces on the planet which are required to be kept inviolate; they defend them from molestation, and with the violet devas are at this time working definitely, though temporarily, under the Lord Maitreya. The Raja Lord of the astral plane, Varuna and his brother Kshiti, have been called to the council chamber of the Hierarchy for specific consultation, and just as the Masters are endeavouring to prepare humanity for service when the World Teacher comes, so these Raja Lords are working along similar lines in connection with the

Effects of the Incoming Seventh Ray

devas. They are arduous in Their work, intense in Their zeal, but much obstructed by man.

The white devas of the air and water who preside over the atmosphere work with certain aspects of electrical phenomena, and control the seas, rivers, and streams. From among them, at a certain stage in their evolution, are gathered the guardian angels of the race when in physical plane incarnation. Each unit of the human family has his guardian deva.

Each group of devas has some specific method of development and some means whereby they evolve and attain a particular goal.

For the *violet* devas the path of attainment lies through feeling, and through educating the race in the perfecting of the physical body in its two departments.

For the *green* devas the path of service is seen in magnetisation, of which the human race knows nothing as yet. Through this power they act as the protectors of the vegetable plant life, and of the sacred spots of the earth; in their work lies the safety of man's body, for from the vegetable kingdom for the remainder of this round comes the nourishment of that body.

For the *white* devas the path of service lies in the guarding of the individuals of the human family, in the care and segregation of types, in the control of the water and air elementals, and much that concerns the fish kingdom.

Thus in the service of humanity in some form or another lies attainment for these physical plane devas. They have much to give and do for humanity, and in time it will be apparent to the human unit what he has to give towards the perfecting of the deva kingdom. A great hastening of their evolution goes forward now coincident with that of the human family.

CF 910-14

It is possible at this time to foretell certain events which will come to pass during the next one hundred years.

First, in about ten years time the first ether, with all that is composed of that matter, will be recognised scientific fact, and the scientists who work intuitively will come to recognise the devas of that plane. People coming into incarnation on this seventh ray will have the eyes that see, and the purple devas and the lesser devas of the etheric body will be visioned by them.

EPI 123

Groups will later be formed for specific purposes, which brings me to my third point, the use of the Word for certain calculated ends.

Let me enumerate for you some of the aims groups will have in view when they form themselves, and by the use of the Sacred Word, coupled to the true occult meditation, achieve certain results. The time for this is not yet, and need arises not for detailed description, yet if things progress as desired, even you may see it somewhat worked out in your lifetime....

7—Groups that definitely work at making contact with the devas, and collaborating with them under the law. During the seventh ray activity, this will be much facilitated.

LOM 67-68

Dangers from the deva evolution

This second point is more complex. You will remember how it has been said earlier in these letters that contact with the devas can be brought about through specific forms and mantrams and that in this contact lies peril for the unwary. This danger is curiously real now, owing to the following reasons:

a.....The coming in of the violet ray, the seventh or Ceremonial Ray, has rendered this contact more easy of attainment than heretofore. It is therefore the ray on which approximation is possible, and in the use of ceremonial and of set forms, coupled to regulated rhythmic movement, will be found a meeting place for the two allied evolutions. In the use of ritual this will be apparent, and psychics are already bearing witness to the fact that both in the ritual of the Church and in that of Masonry this has been evidenced. More and more will this be the case, and it carries with it certain risks that will inevitably work themselves into common knowledge and thus affect in various ways the unwary sons of men. As you know, a definite effort is being made at this time by the Planetary Hierarchy to communicate to the devas their part in the scheme of things, and the part the human family must likewise play. The work is slow, and certain results are inevitable. It is not my purpose to take up with you in these letters the part that ritual and set mantric forms play in the evolution of devas and of men. I only desire to point out that danger for human beings lies in the unwise use of forms for the calling of the devas, in experimenting with the Sacred Word with the object in view of contacting the Builders who are so largely affected by it, and in endeavouring to pry into the secrets of ritual with its adjuncts of colour and of sound. Later on, when the pupil has passed the portal of initiation, such knowledge will be his, coupled with the necessary information that teaches him to work with the law. In the following of the law, no danger lurks.

LOM 128-29

...The lower kingdoms of the devas work, guided by the great Building Devas, and all move upward in ordered beauty from plane to plane, from system to system, universe to universe. Therefore in studying occult lore you need to remember two things:—

a. You control elemental forces.
b. You co-operate with the devas.

In one you dominate, in the other case you endeavour to work with. You control through the activity aspect, by the definite doing of certain things, by the preparation of certain ceremonies, for instance, through which certain forces can play. It is a replica on a tiny miniature scale of what the third Logos did in world making. Certain activities had certain results. Later on, revelations can be made as to the rites and ceremonies through which you can get in touch with the various elementals, and control them. The Ceremonial Ray—by coming into incarnation at this time, is making things much easier along this particular line.

Fire elementals, water sprites, and the lower elementals can all be harnessed by rites. The rites are of three kinds:—

1. Protective rites, which concern your own protection.
2. Rites of appeal, which call and reveal the elementals.
3. Rites that control and direct them when summoned.

In working with the devas you use the *wisdom or love* aspect, the second aspect of the Logos, the building aspect. Through love and longing you reach them and your first step (as you are on the path of evolution, as they are) is to get in touch with them, for together you must work in the future for the guidance of the elemental forces and the helping of humanity. It is not safe for human beings, poor foolish things, to tamper with the forces of involution until they themselves are linked with the devas through purity of character and nobility of soul.

Through rites and ceremonies you can sense the devas and reach them, but not in the same manner nor for the same reason that you can the elementals. The devas attend ceremonies freely and are not summoned; they come, as you do, to tap the power. When your vibrations are pure enough the ceremonies serve as a common meeting-ground.

LOM 175-76

Effects of the Incoming Seventh Ray

The devas of the physical plane, though divided into the three groups A, B, C, are under another grouping spoken of as *"the Devas of the Seventh Order"*. The seventh order is peculiarly linked to the devas of the first order on the first plane. They are the reflectors of the mind of God of which the first order is the expression, and manifest it as it has worked through from the archetypal plane. This seventh order of devas is directly under the influence of the seventh ray, and the planetary Logos of that ray works in close co-operation with the Raja-Lord of the seventh plane. As the goal of evolution for the devas is the inner hearing, it will be apparent why mantric sounds and balanced modulations are the method of contacting them, and of producing varying phenomena. This seventh order of devas is the one with which the workers on the left hand path are concerned, working through vampirism and the devitalisation of their victims. They deal with the etheric bodies of their enemies, and by means of sounds affect deva substance, thus producing the desired results. The white Magician does not work on the physical plane with physical substance. He transfers His activities to a higher level, and hence deals with desires and motives. He works through the devas of the sixth order.

CF 667-68

Spiritualism

The rise of modern spiritualism is no doubt due to the seventh sub-ray influence [of the sixth ray, *Editors*] and it may also be a foreshadowing of the great seventh ray still to come. It is interesting to note that this movement was started by a secret society which has existed in the world since the last period of seventh ray dominance in Atlantean times.

EPI 166-67

Each of the great rays has a form of teaching truth to humanity which is its unique contribution, and in this way develops man by a system or technique which is qualified by the ray quality and is therefore specific and unique. Let me point out to you the modes of this group teaching:....

Ray VII..Higher Expression: All forms of white magic.
        Lower Expression: Spiritualism or "phenomena"....

EPI 49-50

It is through the correct development of spiritualism along psychological lines and the withdrawal of its emphasis upon phenomena (which is its outstanding characteristic and emphasis today) that the true nature of death and of the hereafter will be revealed. But it is in connection with spiritualism that I can best illustrate the lower expression of the incoming seventh ray influences. The work of the seventh ray is, as you know, the relating of life and of form, but when the emphasis is laid upon the form aspect then the wrong procedure eventuates and the work of the black magician can begin, and his objectives come unduly into play. This is what has happened in the spiritualistic movement; its investigators are occupied with the form side of life and its adherents with the satisfaction of their emotional desires (again related to the form side) so that the true import of the movement is in danger of being lost.

Spiritualism, in its lowest and material aspect, is a low grade expression of the seventh ray and is—for the masses—definitely a line of least resistance, and, therefore, of no great spiritual importance to their evolutionary development. The masses of the people are today Atlantean in their consciousness and are only slowly emerging into the Aryan point of view. This must change and the mind activity be rapidly enhanced or else true spiritualism will be unable to express itself and—through the present spiritualistic movement—there can be let loose upon the world forces and entities of a most undesirable character. The negativity of the majority of those who are interested in spiritualism and the entire negativity of the bulk of the mediums throws the door wide open to very definite dangers. Fortunately, there is a movement within spiritualistic circles to right this obvious danger and to shift the present emphasis upon phenomena into the world of true values and right understanding. The subject is too vast a one for me to deal with here, except in illustration of the points which I am endeavouring to make, but one hint I will give. If the societies and organisations, connected with the spiritualistic movement and the psychical research groups, would seek for and find the natural sensitives (and not the trance mediums) and those who are naturally clair-audient and clair-voyant and would study their disclosures, their words, their reactions and their modes of working they would discover much about some of the natural and normal powers of man—powers which have been in abeyance during the period wherein mind development has been the objective and which humanity shares with two great groups of lives—the Members of the Hierarchy and the animal kingdom. Ponder on this. If, therefore, these societies would concentrate on the *intelligent and mental psychics* and rule out all trance conditions it would not be long before revelation would come. The trance condition is undesirable, separates the medium from his soul and definitely relegates him to the realm of the negative, of the uncontrolled and of material forces. This development, however, the forces of materiality will prevent if possible because the moment there is positive intelligent understanding of the world on the other side of the veil, there is no fear of death and then the major aspect of their power and of their hold upon humanity will disappear.

If you have followed intelligently what I have said, two points will emerge with clarity in your minds in relation to the initial and immediate activity of these two rays—the sixth and the seventh. First, that entire groups of people are increasingly susceptible to their influence and this inevitably leads to these groups (responsive to either the sixth or the seventh ray forces) being in opposition to and antagonistic to each other. The problem is that, owing to the developed sensitivity of the race, this antagonism is now upon a world-wide scale. Hence much of the present conflict of ideas, and the opposing ideologies, and hence also the feud between the old inherited traditions and the ancient forms of civilisation, of government, of religion on the one hand and of the newer emerging ideas on the other. These new concepts should usher in the New Age and will eventually revolutionise our modern life and standards. They will relegate the old ideas to the same position as the ideas which governed the race one thousand years ago have today assumed in our consciousness.

Second: The situation is still further complicated by the fact that both these rays influence and express themselves (as is ever the case) in a dual manner and have always a lower and a higher form of manifestation, which is a correspondence in this connection to the personality, and the egoic expression of every human being. In the case of the out-going ray, the higher form (which is ever the first to manifest in germ) is rapidly disappearing or is being absorbed into the newer idealism, thus contributing all that is best to the new presentation of truth so that the emerging culture will be properly rooted in the old. The lower forms are, however, tenacious and dominant and because of this they definitely constitute today the major problem of the Hierarchy, so much so that they require the calling in of the first ray (or the Shamballa force) in order to effect their destruction. Bear this in mind as you study the world situation. The lower forms of the seventh ray expression are still in an embryonic stage. This you can see clearly if you consider the one to which I chose to refer—the spiritualistic movement—which began to take shape only during the last century and has achieved its curiously phenomenal growth only because it started upon the American continent. The United States of America was the centre of old Atlantis and hence inherited a psychic and ancient religious form which was existent and potently alive in that part of the world for many centuries.

In spite of these facts, the higher and more living energy of the seventh ray is the most active at this time and its resultant idealism and consequent New Age concepts are playing upon the sensitive minds of the race and preparing humanity for a great and much needed change. The work of the Ray of Ceremonial Order is to "ground" or make physically visible the results of bringing spirit and matter together. Its function is to clothe spirit with matter, producing form.

DN 43-47

It is harder to differentiate between the higher and the lower expressions of the seventh Ray of Ceremonial Order, for this ray is only in process of manifestation and we know not as yet what its major expressions will be, either higher or lower. Human reactions have their place and—as I have earlier pointed out—even the Masters Themselves do not and cannot foretell what the results of the impacts of force may be nor what may eventuate as a result, though They can frequently determine the probable happenings. If I say to you that the higher expression of the seventh ray is white magic, do you really understand what I mean? I question it. Have you any true idea of what is intended by these two words? I doubt it. White magic is realistically the power of the trained worker and executive to bring together into a constructive synthesis the "within and the without" so that that which is below may be recognisably patterned upon that which is above. It is the supreme task of bringing together in accordance with the immediate intent and plan and for the benefit of the evolving life in any particular world cycle:

1. Spirit and matter.
2. Life and form.
3. The ego and the personality.
4. The soul and its outer expression.
5. The higher worlds of atma—buddhi—manas and the lower reflection of mind—emotion and the physical nature.
6. The head and the heart, through the sublimation of the sacral and the solar plexus energies.
7. The etheric-astral planes and the dense physical plane.
8. The intangible subjective levels of existence and the outer tangible worlds.

Such is the task of the white magician and as evolution proceeds and becomes more complicated and complex it will nevertheless be more rapid and more accurately defined in the mind of the magician. All, therefore, that is conducive to human sensitivity and to increased awareness is the work of the white magician; all that tends to produce better forms through which the living principle of deity can express itself is the work of the white magician; all that serves to thin or tear away the veil between the worlds wherein those who have no physical bodies live and move and work and the worlds of outer form is the work of the white magician. Of all this type of work there is always much, but never more so than at this time owing to the coming into manifestation of this ray of the magician (black and white), the seventh ray. Hence the rapid growth of the sense of omnipresence and the recognition of the non-existence of time in relation to reality. This has taken place through the discovery and use of the radio and of the many means of communication and through the steady growth of telepathic interplay; hence also the spread of education, enlarging man's horizon and opening up to him new worlds for investigation and adventure; hence also the breaking down of the old and limiting forms through the invoked force of the first ray, which has hitherto always worked through the medium of the seventh ray, because the kingdoms in nature cannot yet stand pure first ray energy; hence also the keen interest in the life after death and the appearance of all the many groups which are today investigating the nature of survival and the probability of immortality; hence again the appearance of the modern spiritualistic movement. This is a direct effect of the coming into manifestation of the seventh ray. Spiritualism was the religion of old Atlantis and the seventh ray dominated that ancient civilisation for a very long period of time, particularly during the first half of its existence, just as the fifth ray is of such dominant potency in our Aryan age and race.

DN 41-43

Future Unfoldment: The Fusion of Spirit and Matter

White magic—as I would have you remember—is concerned with the unfoldment of the soul in form and its gaining needed experience thereby. It is not concerned with direct work upon the form but with the indirect influence of the soul, functioning in any form in every kingdom in nature as it brings the form under its control, thereby effecting needed and developing changes in the apparatus of contact. The white magician knows that when the proper and correct ray stimulation is applied to the centre which we call the soul in any form but not to the form itself, that then the soul, thus stimulated, will do its own work of destruction, of attraction, of rebuilding and of a consequent renewed life manifestation. This is true of the soul of man, of the soul of a nation and of the soul of humanity itself. Bear this in mind, for I have here stated a basic and fundamental rule by which all white magic is agelessly governed.

It is for this reason that the seventh ray is spoken of as governing the mineral kingdom and also as manifesting through its mediumship that significant soul characteristic and quality which we call radiation. That word effectively describes the result of soul stimulation upon and within every form. The life of the soul eventually radiates beyond the form and this radiation produces definite and calculated effects. The sixth ray is, as you know, very closely related to the animal kingdom and its effect there is to produce in the higher forms of animal life the quality and expression of domesticity, and the adaptability of the animal to human contact. The rays controlling the animal kingdom are the seventh, the third and the sixth. Hence you can easily see that the relation which exists between the higher animals and man is a ray relation and, therefore, useful under the evolutionary law and inevitable in its results. The rays governing the vegetable kingdom are the sixth, the second and the fourth and here again there is an inter-locking relation through the medium of the sixth ray. The human kingdom is governed by the fourth, the fifth and again the fourth and this again indicates relationship. Some day these relations and inter-connected lines of force will be better understood and scientifically studied and the lines of related energies investigated. This inter-locking directorate of energies will engage the attention of some of the best minds and when that takes place much will be learnt. This information is, however, of negligible use at this time and will remain so until such time as men are sensitive to the vibration of the different rays and can isolate a ray rhythm in their consciousness. When this sensitivity is developed, then many rapid, significant and revolutionary discoveries will be made.

One of the inevitable effects of seventh ray energy will be to relate and weld into a closer synthesis the four kingdoms in nature. This must be done as preparatory to the long fore-ordained work of humanity which is to be the distributing agency for spiritual energy to the three subhu-

Effects of the Incoming Seventh Ray

man kingdoms. This is the major task of service which the fourth kingdom, through its incarnating souls, has undertaken. The radiation from the fourth kingdom will some day be so potent and far-reaching that its effects will permeate down into the very depths of the created phenomenal world, even into the mineral kingdom. Then we shall see the results to which the great initiate, Paul, refers when he speaks of the whole creation waiting for the manifestation of the Sons of God. That manifestation is that of radiating glory and power and love.

DN 122-24

...It might be useful here to remember that in the work of creation the white magician avails himself *of the current ray influence.* When the third, fifth and seventh rays are in power, either coming in, at full meridian, or passing out, the work is much easier than when the second, sixth or fourth are dominant. At the present time, the seventh ray, as we know, is rapidly dominating, and it is one of the easiest forces with which man has to work. Under this ray it will be possible to build a new structure for the rapidly decaying civilisation, and to erect the new temple desired for the religious impulse. Under its influence the work of the numerous unconscious magicians will be much facilitated. This will eventuate in the rapid growth of unconscious psychic phenomena, in the spread of mental science, and the consequent ability of thinkers to acquire and to create those tangible benefits they desire. Nevertheless, this magic of the unconscious or selfish kind leads to karmic results of a deplorable nature, for only those who work with the law and who control the lesser lives through knowledge, love and will, evade the consequences entailed on those who manipulate living matter for selfish ends.

CF 1021-22

The blue ray of devotion passes now into the violet of what we term the ceremonial ray. What do these words mean? Simply that the great Musician of the universe is moving the keys, is sounding another note and thus bringing in another turn of the wheel, and swinging into the arc of manifestation the ray of violet, the great note G. These rays bring with them—in every kingdom in nature—all that is attuned to them: Human beings, devas of order high or low, elementals of a desirable or undesirable nature, flowers, fruits, and vegetable life of a certain kind, and animals and forms of varying species. It is the passing out of a ray that signals the ultimate extinction of some particular form, some type of animal life, and leads to some vegetable aspect coming to an end. Hence the confusion among the scientists at this time. The process of coming in is slow, as is all work in nature, and as is the process of passing out. Simultaneously with the cyclic birth and emergence of a new ray is the slow return to its source of the prevailing ray, present at the advent of the new.

At this time the sixth ray is passing out and is taking with it all those forms whose keynote is blue—those people, for instance, who with devotion (misplaced or not) followed some particular object, person or idea. With it passes, therefore, those whom we term fanatics, those who with one-pointed zeal work towards some sensed objective. Many of the flowers in which you now rejoice are passing out, the bluebell, the hyacinth and the olive for example; the sapphire will become scarce and the turquoise will lose its hue. Flowers of violet colour, of lavender and of purple will come into favour. Behind all this lies a purpose profound.

The physical plane, in its densest aspect, holds little of mystery for man today; he has knowledge on these matters. But the rarer levels of the physical plane lie hid and are, for man, his next field of discovery. The ceremonial ray brings with it the means whereby that knowledge may be acquired and revealed to all, and thus not be the sole property of the wise and of the occultists. The three higher etheric levels, with their denizens, are waiting to become the property of all, and with their inhabitants comes the next approximation.

EPI 121-23

[Regarding the esoteric meaning of the exoteric colours] only four as yet can be communicated, but if rightly understood they hold the key to the present fourth round, and to its history. This being the fourth chain and the fourth round you will note therefore how in the number four lies the history of the present. Especially would I urge you who are the teachers and students of the coming generation to ponder upon the significance of white being esoterically violet. It has special application now in the coming in of the violet ray, the seventh ray being one of the three major rays *in this round*; it wields power in ratio to the four, on the four and under the four.

LOM 224

We live today in a period of the world's history wherein three events of major importance are taking place, mostly unrealised and unobserved by the majority of people.

The seventh Ray of Law and Order is coming into manifestation; we are transiting into a new sign of the zodiac, and the "coming of Christ" is imminent. These three great happenings are the cause of much of the present upheaval and chaos; at the same time they are responsible for the universal turning to spiritual realities which all true workers at this time recognise, and for the growth of understanding, of welfare movements and of the tendency to cooperation, of religious unity and of internationalism. Types of energy which have hitherto been latent are now becoming potent. The consequent world reaction is, in the initial stages, material in its manifestation; in its final stages, divine qualities will manifest and change history and civilisation. The interest being shown today in the so-called cosmic rays indicates a scientific recognition of the new incoming seventh ray energies. These rays, pouring through the sacral centre of the planetary etheric body, have necessarily an effect upon the sacral centres of humanity, and hence the sex life of mankind is temporarily over-stimulated, and hence also the present over-emphasis upon sex. But hence also (and this must be remembered) the keen impetus now being mentally expressed which will eventually result in man's thinking through to a solution of this problem of sex.

The coming in of the Aquarian age also stimulates in man a spirit of universality and a tendency towards fusion. This can be seen working out in the present trend towards synthesis in business, in religion and in politics. It produces an urge towards union, and among other unions, towards religious understanding and tolerance. But these influences, playing upon the sensitive bodies of the undeveloped and the over-psychic, lead to a morbid tendency towards unions, legitimate and illegitimate; they produce an extreme aptitude to sexual intercourse in many directions, and to relations and fusions which are not along the intended or the evolutionary line, and which outrage oft the very laws of nature itself. Energy is an impersonal thing, and is dual in its effect—the effect varying according to the type of substance upon which it plays.

The incoming seventh ray expresses the power to organise, the ability to integrate and to bring into synthetic relation the great pairs of opposites, and thus produce the new forms of spiritual manifestation. But it will also produce the new forms of what, from the standpoint of spirit, may be regarded as material evil. It is the great impulse which will bring into the light of day all that is to be found clothed with matter, and will thus eventually lead to the revelation of spirit and of the hidden glory, when that which has been revealed of the material form has been purified and sanctified. This it was to which Christ referred when He prophesied that, at the end of the age, the hidden things would be made plain, and secrets be shouted from the housetops.

By means of this process of revelation, within the human family as well as elsewhere in nature, we shall have the development of the power of thought. This will come about through the development of the faculty of discrimination, which will offer choices to man, and thus develop a truer sense of values. False and true standards will emerge in man's consciousness, and those choices will be made which will lay the foundation of the new order, which will inaugurate the new race, with its new laws and novel approaches, and so usher in the new religion of love and brotherhood, and that period wherein the group and the group-good will be the dominant note. Then separateness and hatreds will fade out and men will be merged in a true unity.

The third factor under consideration, the coming of the Christ as it is called, must also be noted. Everywhere we find the spirit of expectancy, and the demand for a manifestation and a symbolic happening which we call by various names but which is usually referred to as the advent of Christ. This, as you know, may be an actual physical coming, as before in Palestine, or it may connote a definite over-shadowing of His disciples and lovers by the Great Lord of Life. This over-shadowing will call forth a response from all those who are in any way spiritually awakened. Or again, the coming may take the form of a tremendous inflow of the Christ principle, the Christ life and love, working out through the human family. Perhaps all three possibilities may be found simultaneously on our planet very shortly. It is not for us to say. It is for us to be ready, and for us to work at preparing the world for that significant series of events. The immediate future will show. The point I seek to make, however, is that this inflow of the Christ spirit of love (whether it comes through a Person in bodily form or through His felt and realised Presence) will again be two-fold in its effect.

This is a hard saying for the unthinking and the illogical. Both the good and the evil man will be stimulated; both material desire and spiritual aspiration will be awakened and fostered. Facts prove the truth of the saying that a heavily fertilised garden and a carefully tended and watered plot of ground will produce its crop of weeds as well as flowers. Yet in this fact you have two reactions to the same sun, the same water, the same fertilising agency and the same care. The difference exists in the seeds found in the ground upon which these factors play. The inflow of love therefore will stimulate earthly love and earthly desire and animal lust; it will foster the urge to possess in the material sense, with all the evil consequent upon this attitude, and the resulting growth of sexual reactions, and the many expressions of an ill-regulated mechanism, responding to an impersonal force. But it will also produce the growth of brotherly love and foster the development and the expression of group consciousness, of universal understanding; it will produce a new and powerful tendency to fusion, to at-one-ment and to synthesis. All this will be brought about through the medium of humanity and the Christ spirit. Steadily the love of Christ will be shed abroad in the earth, and its influence will grow stronger during the coming centuries, until at the end of the Aquarian age, and through the work of the seventh ray (bringing the pairs of opposites into closer cooperation), we can look for the "raising of Lazarus from the dead", and the emergence of humanity out of the tomb of matter. The hidden divinity will be revealed. Steadily all forms will be brought

Effects of the Incoming Seventh Ray

under the influence of the Christ spirit, and the consummation of love will be brought about.

EPI 279-83

Violet. In a curious way the violet Ray of Ceremonial Law or Order is a synthetic ray when manifested in the three worlds. Just as the synthetic Ray of Love and Wisdom is the synthesis of all the *life* forces, so in the three worlds the seventh ray synthesises all that has to do with *form.* On the first plane, life in its purest, highest, undifferentiated synthetic aspect; on the seventh plane, form in its densest, grossest, most differentiated aspect; one is summed up in the synthetic Ray of Love, whilst the other is worked upon by the seventh.

A synthesis too is found in the fact that through the medium of violet the deva and human kingdoms can find a place of contact. Esoterically violet is white. In the blending of these two kingdoms the seven Heavenly Men attain perfection and completeness, and are esoterically considered to be white, the synonym of perfection.

Another point of synthesis is the fact that through the dominance of this seventh ray comes a point of merging between the dense physical and the etheric bodies. This is of paramount importance in the macrocosm, and to the student of meditation. It is necessary to effect this merging and alignment before the transmission of the teaching to the dense physical brain can in any way be considered accurate. It has a close bearing upon the alignment of the centres.

LOM 221-22

At the sounding of the seventh subtone crystallisation occurred and absolute conformity to the law of approach. It resulted in the dense aspect of manifestation, the point of deepest experience. You will note its connection, therefore, with the Ray of Ceremonial Law, one of the great building rays—a ray which adjusts matter, under set forms, to the desired shapes.

LOM 56

Ray Avatars. These great Beings come forth at relatively long intervals when a ray is coming into manifestation. They embody the quality and the force of a particular ray. Next century, when the seventh ray has achieved complete manifestation and the Piscean influence is entirely removed, the seventh ray Avatar will appear. His work will demonstrate the law, order and rhythm of the creative process as it works out on the physical plane, blending spirit and matter. And as this ray is called the Ray of Ceremonial Order or Ritual, He will be largely instrumental in producing those conditions which will permit of the reappearance upon Earth of the Mysteries of Initiation, of which the Hierarchy is the custodian. He is necessarily connected with the Great White Lodge on Sirius. This fact does not, however, concern us now, for we await the coming of a still greater Avatar.

EXH 298-99

We might consider the effect of this incoming force [the seventh ray, *Editors*] along three lines:

First. The type of force, or the logoic quality, with its function and aim.

Second. Its work in relation to:
   a. The animal kingdom.
   b. The human kingdom.
   c. The deva kingdom.

Third. The results to be looked for during the coming centuries.

The type of force, or the nature of the Heavenly Man of the seventh ray, is fundamentally constructive. It will be necessary here to touch somewhat upon His character and

His place in the logoic scheme, calling attention to the need of refraining from personalisation and externalisation. The Heavenly Man of the scheme in which the Ray of Ceremonial Magic is embodied is one of the main transmitters of radiation from the Sun to the system and has a close connection with logoic kundalini. Herein lies a hint. The Raja-Lord of the etheric levels of the physical plane works in close alliance with Him and this will be apparent if we bear in mind that the Lord of a plane is its embodied activity. He is the energising force that expresses itself as a unified Identity in the matter of a plane, and we might therefore get some idea of the coherency of Their mutual work if we bear in mind that

> The Raja-Lord of a plane is the sum total of the substance of that plane.
>
> The planetary Logos Who is most closely connected with any particular plane is its quality and colouring.

By the united action and work of these two Entities all is accomplished—the Lord of the Builders constructing the forms which the Lord of Life utilises to develop consciousness within.

The force or vibration of any ray might be summed up as:

a. The intelligent purpose of an Entity, a planetary Logos.

b. His life energy working in, through, and upon His body of manifestation.

c. His magnetic radiation as it affects (though in lesser degree) His Brothers in manifestation.

d. His peculiar colouring or quality, His main psychological aspect, demonstrating through His own activities within His own scheme.

e. The effect of the same as it influences His Brothers within the body corporate of the solar Logos.

f. His life force as it radiates beyond His own periphery as active energy and stimulating activity—being literally one of the aspects of Fohat. The activity aspect of a Heavenly Man is as much an aspect of Fohat as Brahma is the sumtotal of Fohat. The Heavenly Men are, by virtue of physical manifestation, Fohat and His Brothers.

When this is borne in mind it will be seen that each of the planetary Logoi, equally with a solar Logos, and with Their reflections, human beings, demonstrate through the aspects.

In their totality all these are the expression of the incarnating Logos; in the one case His fohatic energy builds the kingdoms of nature, giving them Body; in the other He gives them their psychical value, and finally through them all He demonstrates as Existence or Being.

Similar tables can be worked out for a Heavenly Man and a human being, laying the emphasis always upon the development of the middle or psychic aspect.

With these thoughts in mind it should be possible to see more clearly what the coming in of a ray, such as the present one, or its passing out, may involve. In the particular case under discussion, we have the coming in of a ray that is intimately connected with the plane of manifestation, the physical plane, which is (within the greater cycle) responsible for man's very existence, and the source of his future hope.

This seventh ray (fifth) ever manifests in a period of transition from one kingdom to another, and this holds hid the mystery of the particular form of service of its planetary Logos. He governs the processes of:

Transmutation
Incarnation
Transference.

Effects of the Incoming Seventh Ray

In these three words His life-work is summed up; in these three words is embodied the nature of this great Entity, Who presides over the processes of blending and merging and adaptation; Who, through His knowledge of cosmic Sound, guides the life forces of certain solar and lunar entities from form to form, and is the link between the soul awaiting incarnation, and its body of manifestation. This is equally true whether we are considering the incarnation of a man, of a group, of an idea, or of all entities of lesser grade to the solar Being Who manifests through a globe, or the regent of the globe under the planetary Logos. All entities of higher rank than this great evolutionary Being come into incarnation through the linking work of an extra-systemic Being. In all periods of the transference of the life from

System to system,
Scheme to scheme,
Chain to chain,

this cosmic Deity pours forth His power and influence. In all periods of lesser transition of the life from

Globe to globe,
Plane to plane,
Kingdom of nature to another kingdom,

the Lord of the seventh ray plays a similar part.

Herein lies the reason for His inflowing force at this time, for a profound movement is in order of accomplishment, and a transference is in progress which calls for His particular type of energy. A transference is being effected of certain groups of human and deva Monads out of the human kingdom into the fifth or spiritual kingdom. During His cycle of close on two thousand five hundred years, a specific number of men will pass on to the Path of Initiation, and take at least the first Initiation, thus transferring their centres of consciousness out of the purely human into the early stages of the spiritual.

During this same cycle, a transference of units from out of the animal kingdom into the human will proceed in the fifth chain and from thence onto another chain, thus producing a period of even greater activity than on our own globe. Similarly I may point out (even though it is not possible to give more than a hint) that the force of the cosmic Transferrer is being called into activity by the transference during this cycle of a special group of highly advanced units of the human and deva kingdoms (members of the occult Hierarchy) to another scheme altogether. Certain units also—from among the Lipika Lords—are taking advantage of this cosmic influence to transfer their activity to another system, giving place to others Who will work out the karma of the new age. The power of these agencies permeates the entire globe and extends throughout the chains and schemes which lie in the line of its path. It will fundamentally affect the vegetable kingdom, obscuring old types and bringing in new; it will work in the mineral kingdom and give a new impetus to the chemical processes, causing incidentally a setting loose of radioactive units, and a consequent accretion of knowledge by the scientist. In the elemental kingdoms and the group souls found therein, it produces facility in the transference of atoms.

So far-reaching are the effects of this ray, both on the deva and human units in their different kingdoms that entirely new environments will evolve for the utilisation of the new types and entirely new characteristics will be found emerging in the race of men.

We have somewhat considered the type of force which expresses itself by means of the seventh ray and have seen that it is the great transmuting, and transferring agent of the Logos. We have seen that it has a powerful effect both on deva and human units; we have found that the prime function of the Logos of the seventh Ray is beyond all else, that of adaptation, or the moulding of the form and the building rays—a ray which adjusts matter, under set forms, to the desired shapes.

LOM 56

Ray Avatars. These great Beings come forth at relatively long intervals when a ray is coming into manifestation. They embody the quality and the force of a particular ray. Next century, when the seventh ray has achieved complete manifestation and the Piscean influence is entirely removed, the seventh ray Avatar will appear. His work will demonstrate the law, order and rhythm of the creative process as it works out on the physical plane, blending spirit and matter. And as this ray is called the Ray of Ceremonial Order or Ritual, He will be largely instrumental in producing those conditions which will permit of the reappearance upon Earth of the Mysteries of Initiation, of which the Hierarchy is the custodian. He is necessarily connected with the Great White Lodge on Sirius. This fact does not, however, concern us now, for we await the coming of a still greater Avatar.

EXH 298-99

We might consider the effect of this incoming force [the seventh ray, *Editors*] along three lines:

First. The type of force, or the logoic quality, with its function and aim.

Second. Its work in relation to:
   a. The animal kingdom.
   b. The human kingdom.
   c. The deva kingdom.

Third. The results to be looked for during the coming centuries.

The type of force, or the nature of the Heavenly Man of the seventh ray, is fundamentally constructive. It will be necessary here to touch somewhat upon His character and under the influence of the Christ spirit, and the consummation of love will be brought about.

EPI 279-83

Violet. In a curious way the violet Ray of Ceremonial Law or Order is a synthetic ray when manifested in the three worlds. Just as the synthetic Ray of Love and Wisdom is the synthesis of all the *life* forces, so in the three worlds the seventh ray synthesises all that has to do with *form*. On the first plane, life in its purest, highest, undifferentiated synthetic aspect; on the seventh plane, form in its densest, grossest, most differentiated aspect; one is summed up in the synthetic Ray of Love, whilst the other is worked upon by the seventh.

A synthesis too is found in the fact that through the medium of violet the deva and human kingdoms can find a place of contact. Esoterically violet is white. In the blending of these two kingdoms the seven Heavenly Men attain perfection and completeness, and are esoterically considered to be white, the synonym of perfection.

Another point of synthesis is the fact that through the dominance of this seventh ray comes a point of merging between the dense physical and the etheric bodies. This is of paramount importance in the macrocosm, and to the student of meditation. It is necessary to effect this merging and alignment before the transmission of the teaching to the dense physical brain can in any way be considered accurate. It has a close bearing upon the alignment of the centres.

LOM 221-22

At the sounding of the seventh subtone crystallisation occurred and absolute conformity to the law of approach. It resulted in the dense aspect of manifestation, the point of deepest experience. You will note its connection, therefore, with the Ray of Ceremonial Law, one of the great

The coming into incarnation of numbers of old magicians and occultists and the rapid growth therefore of recognised psychic powers among the people. This psychism, being tinged with mentality and not being of a purely astral quality, will be even more dangerous than in Atlantean days, for back of it will be some degree of will, conscious purpose, and intellectual apprehension, and unless this is paralleled by the growth of spiritual realisation, and by the steady grip of the Ego upon the lower personality, a period of real danger may ensue. Hence the need of pointing out and of realising the menace, so that the truth of the inner life and the need of serving the race as an essential to advancement may be proclaimed far and wide.

Paralleling the incoming of this large band of seventh ray magicians (some linked to the brotherhood and some to the purely manasic groups) is the proposed advent of certain members of the Hierarchy (initiates below the fourth Initiation) and of certain disciples and probationers, all on this ray and all true psychics, who hope through their endeavours to offset the vibrations, and ward off the menace incident to the advent of the other group. The arranging of this and the preparing of the way for them in the different countries, especially in Europe and North America, is occupying the attention at this time of the Master R— and the Master H—.

A group of scientists will come into incarnation on the physical plane during the next seventy-five years who will be the medium for the revelation of the next three truths concerning electrical phenomena. A formula of truth concerning this aspect of manifestation was prepared by initiates on the fifth ray at the close of the last century, being part of the usual attempt of the Hierarchy to promote evolutionary development at the close of every cycle of one hundred years. Certain parts (two fifths) of that formula have worked out through the achievements of such men as Edison and those who participate in his type of endeavour, and through the work of those who have dealt with the subject of radium and radioactivity. Three more parts of the same formula have still to come, and will embody all that it is possible or safe for man to know anent the physical plane manifestation of electricity during the fifth subrace.

All that we have here considered covers the time till the coming in of the new subrace. This race will summarise and carry to a temporary conclusion the manasic effort of the fifth rootrace of mental growth, and will cause results of stupendous import. During the sixth subrace, the emphasis will not be so much on the *development* of mind, as it will be on the *utilisation* of the concrete mind, and its acquired faculty, for the development of the powers of abstract thought. Perhaps too much importance has been attached to the statement of some occult writers that the sixth subrace will be intuitive. The intuition will be awakening, and will be more prominent than now, but the outstanding characteristic will be the ability of the units of the sixth subrace to think in abstract terms, and to use the abstract mind. Their function will be to perfect (as far as may be in this round) the group antaskarana, or the link between the mental and buddhic. This bridge will be of a usable nature during the sixth rootrace in which the intuition will show real and general signs of existing. In this rootrace, units only show signs here and there of real intuition, having built the necessary bridge in their individual selves. In the sixth rootrace small groups will be intuitive.

It is needless to say more here anent the influence of the seventh ray upon the sons of men. More later may be available but enough has been suggested to form the basis of useful speculation.

CF 452-57

The Seventh Seed Group

The work of the seventh group, which is in the field of science, is closely allied to that of the seventh ray and is one with a most practical physical purpose. It is strictly magical in its technique, and this technique is intended to produce a synthesis between the three aspects of divinity upon the physical plane, or between life, the solar energies and the lunar forces. This involves a difficult task and much understanding; the work to be done is not easy to comprehend. It will be carried forward by first ray workers, assisted by seventh ray aspirants, but using fifth ray methods. They will thus combine, in their personnel, the work of the destroyer of outgrown forms, the findings of the scientists who penetrated behind the outer form to its motivating energy, and the practical work of the magician who—under the law—creates the new forms, as expressions of the inflowing life.

This group of disciples will make a close study of the problem of evil, and they will bring about a better understanding of the *purpose* existing in matter or substance, and the inflowing enlightened and different purpose of the soul aspect. That is why (in my earlier discussion of the subject) I linked the results of religion and of science together; religion is concerned with the awakening to conscious purpose of the soul in man or form, whilst science is concerned with the activity of the outer form as it lives its own life, yet slowly becomes subservient to that purpose and to soul impress. This is the thought contained in the words "scientific service" as used by me. The work of this group is therefore a triple one:

1. They will take the most advanced inferences of the workers in the field of science, and will then formulate the new hypotheses upon which the next immediate steps forward in any particular scientific field will be founded.

2. They will avail themselves of the sensitive reactions

which the new spiritual Approaches (as taught by the world religion of the time) will have made possible and—utilising the inferences thus made available in connection with the inner world of spirit—will outline the nature of the incoming forces which will determine and motivate the culture of the time.

3. Taking the substance or material, and the spiritual inferences and the scientific hypotheses, they will formulate those forms of service on the physical plane which will precipitate with rapidity the Plan for the immediate present. They will release through this blend of scientific knowledge and intuitive idealism, those energies which will further human interests, relate the subhuman to the human through a right interplay of forces, and thus clear the way of those intellectual impediments which will (and always have) blocked man's approach to the superhuman world.

EXH 56-57

Work on the etheric body, however, from the standpoint of the Hierarchy is not confined only to the bodies of men. It is a planetary process. The etheric body of the earth itself is being subjected to a definite stimulation. The spirit of the earth, that mysterious entity—not the planetary Logos—is being vivified in a new sense and in his vivification many interesting developments eventuate. In three ways this is being attempted:

1. By an increased rate of vibration of the etheric atoms, caused by the coming in of the ceremonial ray. This must not be pictured as a sudden and violent change. From the standpoint of the human student the rate of increase is apparently so slow and gradual as to be inappreciable. Nevertheless, the stimulation exists, and in the course of centuries will be recognised.

2. By the play of certain astral forces on the etheric body that leads to slow but definite changes in the internal

structure of the atom, the coming into consciousness of another of the spirillae and a general tightening up of the whole cosmos of the atom.

3. By the use on the inner planes by the Mahachohan of one of the powerful talismans of the seventh ray.

The spirit of the earth, it might be noted, is of slow and gradual arousing. He is on the involutionary arc and passes on to the evolutionary in some dim and distant future. Therefore, he will not carry us with him. He but serves our purpose now, offering us a home within his body, yet remaining dissociated from us. The devas of the ethers from this very stimulation are consequently hastening forward in evolution and approximating also nearer to their ideal.

In all I have said anent the etheric body of men, anent the planet, anent the spirit of the earth, the crux of the whole situation lies in the fact that the five rays at this time have the seventh ray as their predominating ray. The seventh ray is the ray that controls the etheric and the devas of the ethers. It controls the seventh sub-plane of all planes but it dominates at this time the seventh sub-plane of the physical plane. Being in the fourth round also, when a ray comes into definite incarnation, it not only controls on planes of the same number but has a special influence on the fourth sub-plane. Note how this works at this time in the three worlds:

1. The fourth ether, the lowest of the ethers, is to be the next physical plane of consciousness. Etheric matter is even now becoming visible to some, and will be entirely visible at the end of this century to many.

2. The fourth sub-plane of the astral holds the majority of men when they pass over and consequently much work on the greatest number can therefore be accomplished.

3. The fourth mental sub-plane is the plane of devachan.

WM 372-74

It might be wise here to elucidate somewhat the idea underlying ceremonial and ritual. There is so much revolt at this time against ceremonial, and so many good and well-meaning people regard themselves as having outgrown and transcended ritual. They pride themselves on having attained that so-called "liberation", forgetting that it is only the sense of individuality that permits this attitude, and that no group work is ever possible without some form of ritual. The refusal therefore to participate in uniformity of action is no sign of a liberated soul.

The Great White Brotherhood has its rituals, but they are rituals which have for their objective the inauguration and the assistance of various aspects of the Plan, and of the varying cyclic activities of that Plan. Where these rituals exist, but where the meaning (inherently present) remains hidden and unrealised, there must as a consequence be demonstrated a spirit of deadness, of uselessness, and of weariness of interest over forms and ceremonies. But where it is demonstrated that ritual and organised ceremonies are but the evidence of a custody of forces and energies, then the idea is constructive in its working out, cooperation with the Plan becomes possible, and the aim of all the divine service begins to demonstrate. All service is governed by ritual.

The coming in of the seventh ray will lead to this desired consummation, and the mystics who are training themselves in the technique of occult motive and in the methods of the trained magician will increasingly find themselves cooperating intelligently with the Plan, and participating in those basic rituals which are distinguished by their power to:

a. Harness the forces of the planet to the service of the race.
b. Send forth those energies which will produce in some one or other of the kingdoms of nature effects of a

desirable and beneficent aspect.
c. Call in and re-distribute the energies which are present in all the forms in the various subhuman kingdoms.
d. Heal through a scientific method of bringing together soul and body.
e. Produce illumination through right understanding of the energy of Light.
f. Evolve that coming ritual which will eventually reveal the true significance of water, which will revolutionise its uses and open to man the free passage to the astral plane. This plane is that of the emotional-desire nature, and its symbol is water. The coming Aquarian Age will reveal to man (and hence also facilitate the work of the seventh ray) that that plane is his natural home at this stage of development. The masses today are entirely, but unconsciously, polarised on that plane. They must become consciously aware of their activity. Man is on the verge of becoming normally awake on the astral plane, and it will be through scientific rituals that this new development will be brought about.

The sixth ray influence produced the appearance of the modern science of psychology, and that science has been its consummating glory. The seventh ray influence will carry forward that infant science to maturity. Belief in the soul has become widespread during the sixth ray period. Knowledge of the soul will be the result of the incoming ray activity, plus the aid contributed by the energies released during the incoming Aquarian Age.

The new and esoteric psychology will be steadily developed. It will be apparent therefore that *A Treatise on White Magic* has a definitely seventh ray import, and this *Treatise on the Seven Rays* has also been sent forth in an effort to clarify the incoming spiritual influences. One of the first lessons that humanity will learn under the potent influence of the seventh ray is that the soul controls its instrument, the personality, through ritual, or through the imposition of a regular rhythm, for rhythm is what really designates a ritual. When aspirants to discipleship impose a rhythm on their lives they call it a discipline, and they feel happy about it. What groups do who are gathered together for the performance of any ritual or ceremony whatsoever (Church ritual, the Masonic work, the drill of the army or navy, business organisations, the proper functioning of a home, of a hospital, or of an entertainment, etc.) is of an analogous nature, for it imposes on the participants a simultaneous performance, an identical undertaking, or a ritual. No one on this earth can evade ritual or ceremonial, for the rising and the setting of the sun imposes a ritual, the cyclic passing of the years, the potent movements of the great centres of population, the coming and the going of trains, of ocean liners and of mails, and the regular broadcasting of the radio organisations—all of these impose a rhythm upon humanity, whether this is recognised or not. Of these rhythms the present great experiments in national standardisation and regimentation are also an expression, as they demonstrate through the masses in any nation.

There is no evading the process of ceremonial living. It is unconsciously recognised, blindly followed, and constitutes the great discipline of the rhythmic breathing of life itself. The Deity works with ritual and is subjected to the ceremonials of the universe. The seven rays come into activity and pass out again under the rhythmic and ritualistic impulse of the divine Life. Thus is the temple of the Lord built by the ceremonial of the Builders. Every kingdom in nature is subjected to ritualistic experience and to the ceremonials of cyclic expression. These only the initiate can comprehend. Every ant hill and every beehive is equally impelled by instinctive rituals and by rhythmic

Effects of the Incoming Seventh Ray 219

impulses. The new science of psychology could well be described as the science of the rituals and rhythms of the body, of the emotional nature and of the mental processes, or of those ceremonials (inherent, innate, or imposed by the self, by circumstances and by environment) which affect the mechanism through which the soul functions.

It is interesting to note how the sixth ray, which produced in human beings the sense of separativeness and of pronounced individualism, has prepared the way for the organising power of the seventh ray. It is almost as if (to speak symbolically) the executives who were to undertake the reorganising of the world in preparation for the New Age were trained and prepared for their task by the influence now going out. Today a process of house-cleaning is going forward in practically every great nation, preparatory to the coming revelation, and the executives and dictators who are sponsoring this realignment and readjustment are the experts whom the genius of each nation has brought forth to deal with the unique problems with which it is beset. They are predominantly seventh ray executives, whose task it is to reorganise the world as a whole upon the newer lines. They are in the nature of material efficiency experts who have been sent in to deal with internal affairs and to institute that activity which will eliminate those factors which prevent the nation concerned from functioning as a whole, as a unit, integrated and coherent. It is from the lack of internal harmony and synthesis that those internal difficulties and disorders emerge which (if of long continuance) prevent a nation having aught to contribute to the world of nations and lead to that nation's being so intensely disordered that the wrong people come into power and the wrong aspects of truth become emphasised. A disordered inharmonious national unit is a menace to the comity of nations, and therefore the separative house-cleanings and rearrangements must go forward before the Federation of Nations can be an accomplished fact.

The new era is however upon its way, and nothing can prevent that which the stars decree and which the Hierarchy of guiding Minds consequently foresee. The new executives who will succeed the present dictators and powers will take over the control towards the year 1955, and they will be seventh ray aspirants and disciples in the majority of cases; their capacity towards integration and towards fusion along right lines will then rapidly bring about the needed international understanding.

The question emerges in your mind as to whether such a prophecy will indeed be fulfilled; and if unfulfilled, will not that fact militate against much that I have said and prove me unreliable? Let me answer this question by pointing out that those of us who foresee that which may and ought to be are nevertheless well aware that though the fulfillment of the prophecy is inevitable, yet the time factor may not work out as indicated. This will be because the distressed human mechanisms of those to whom the work is given will fail to react either correctly or at the right time. These incoming seventh ray aspirants and disciples may make mistakes and may perform their undertakings in such a manner that delay may eventuate. They are permitted to have the general outline of their task committed to them by their own souls, working under the inspiration of those great and liberated souls we call the Masters of the Wisdom, but there is no coercion under the Plan and no forced and dictated service. Much of the success in the coming momentous years is dependent upon the work done by all who may be affiliated (even slightly) with the New Group of World Servers. If public opinion is educated in the new ideals, the momentum of that growing tide will greatly facilitate the work of these seventh ray executives, and in some cases will constitute for them the line of least resistance. Failure, therefore, will rest upon the shoulders of the world aspirants and disciples, and will not indicate inaccurate prophecy or misinterpreted astrological conditions. In any case, the prophesied end is inevitable, but the time of that end rests in the hands of awakened humanity. The margin of difference will also be only between one hundred and three hundred years. The impulse towards synthesis is now too strong to be long delayed....

The prime cosmic function of the seventh ray is to perform the magical work of blending spirit and matter in order to produce the manifested form through which the life will reveal the glory of God. Students would be well advised to pause here and re-read the section of this treatise (see pages 85-86 EPI) in which I dealt with the seventh ray Lord, with His names, and with His purpose. When this has been done, it will be apparent that one of the results of the intensified new influence will be the recognition, by science, of certain effects and characteristics of the work being accomplished. This can already be seen in the work done by scientists in connection with the mineral world. As we have seen in an earlier part of this book, the mineral kingdom is governed by the seventh ray, and to the potency of this incoming ray can be attributed the discovery of the radio-activity of matter. The seventh ray expresses itself in the mineral kingdom through the production of radiation, and we shall find that increasingly these radiations (many of which still remain to be discovered) will be noted, their effects understood and their potencies grasped. One point remains as yet unrealised by science, and that is that these radiations are cyclic in their appearance; under the influence of the seventh ray it has been possible for man to discover and work with radium. Radium has always been present, but not always active in such a manner that we were able to detect it. It is under the influence of the incoming seventh ray that its appearance has been made possible, and it is through this same influence that we shall discover new cosmic rays. They too are always present in our universe, but they use the substance of the incoming ray energy as the path along which they can travel to our planet and thus be revealed. It is many thousands of years since what are now studied as the Cosmic Rays (discovered by Millikan) played definitely upon our planet, and at that time the fifth ray was not active as it now is. Therefore scientific knowledge of their activity was not possible.

Other cosmic rays will play upon our earth as this seventh ray activity becomes increasingly active, and the result of their influence will be to facilitate the emergence of the new racial types, and above all else, to destroy the veil or web which separates the world of the seen and tangible from the world of the unseen and the intangible, the astral world. Just as there is a veil called the "etheric web" dividing off the various force centres in the human body, and protecting the head centres from the astral world, so there is a separating web between the world of physical life and the astral world. This will be destroyed, slowly and certainly, by the play of the cosmic rays upon our planet. The etheric web which is found between the centres in the spine, and which is found at the top of the head (protecting the head centre), is destroyed in man's mechanism by the activity of certain forces found in that mysterious fire which we call the kundalini fire. The cosmic rays of which the modern scientist is aware constitute aspects of the planetary kundalini, and their effect will be the same in the body of the planetary Logos, the Earth, as it is in the human body; the etheric web between the physical and astral planes is in process of destruction, and it is of this event which the sensitives of the world and the spiritualists prophesy as an imminent happening....

Three final points I wish to touch upon. As you may have noted from some of our earlier tabulations, there is a definite relation between the first kingdom in nature, the mineral kingdom, and the final kingdom, the solar kingdom, the seventh and last to appear in manifestation upon our planet. There is a mysterious unity of response existing between the lowest kingdom in the scale of nature and the highest, between that which expresses the densest manifestation of the divine life and that which embodies its final and glorious consummation. This response is fostered by the play of the seventh ray, which produces those initial reactions to organised movement and ritual which, at the close of our great world period, will demonstrate the response of our entire solar system to the same basic seventh ray influence. What can now be seen in the organisation of a crystal, a jewel and a diamond, with their beauty of form and line and colour, their radiance and geometrical perfection, will appear likewise through the medium of the universe as a whole. The Grand Geometrician of the universe works through this seventh ray, and thus sets His seal upon all form life, particularly in the mineral world. This the Masonic Fraternity has always known, and this concept it has perpetuated symbolically in the great world cathedrals, which embody the glory of the mineral world and are the sign of the work of the Master Builder of the universe.

When the great work is consummated we shall see the Temple of God, the solar system, organised objectively and subjectively; its courts and holy places will then be accessible to the sons of men, who will work then without limitation, and will have free access to all parts of the building. Through the magic of the Word, which will then have been recovered, all doors will fly open, and the consciousness of man will respond to every divine manifestation. More of this I may not here say, but the work of the Craft is symbolic of the ritualistic organisation of the universe. Of this the mineral kingdom (with which the work is done, and through which the geometrical plan expresses itself) is at the same time the symbol and the undertaking, the beginning and also the concrete expression of divine purpose.

Secondly, I referred earlier to the work of the seventh ray in connection with the phenomena of electricity, through which the solar system is coordinated and vitalised. There is an aspect of electrical phenomena which produces cohesion, just as there is an aspect which produces light. This has not yet been recognised. It is stated in *The Secret Doctrine* of H.P.B., and in *A Treatise on Cosmic Fire*, that the electricity of the solar system is threefold: there is fire by friction, solar fire, and electric fire—the fire of body, of soul and of spirit. Fire by friction is coming to be somewhat understood by the scientists of the world, and we are harnessing to our needs the fire which heats, which gives light, and which produces motion. This is in the physical sense of the words. One of the imminent discoveries will be the integrating power of electricity as it produces the cohesion within all forms and sustains all form life during the cycle of manifested existence. It produces also the coming together of atoms and of the organisms within forms, so constructing that which is needed to express the life principle. Men today are investigating such matters as electro-therapeutics and studying the theory of the electrical nature of the human being. They are working rapidly towards this coming discovery, and much will be revealed along these lines during the next fifty years. The principle of coordination about which men talk has reference, in the last analysis, to this concept, and the scientific basis of all meditation work is really to be found in this basic truth. The bringing in of force and the offering of a channel are all mystical ways of expressing a natural phenomenon as yet little understood, but which will eventually give the clue to the second aspect of electricity. This will be released in fuller measure during the Aquarian

Effects of the Incoming Seventh Ray

age, through the agency of the seventh ray. One of its earliest effects will be the increase of the understanding of brotherhood and its really scientific basis.

I referred to the fact that man must before long function as freely on the astral plane and through the astral consciousness as he now does on the physical plane. We are today laying the emphasis upon the vital aspect of man; the nature of the life principle is under discussion, and the need for "vital" action everywhere emphasised. We talk of the necessity of increasing human vitality and the vitality of animals and plants; the quality of the vitality-producing factors—food, sun and the coloured rays so widely used now—is creeping slowly into all medical thought, whilst even the advertisers of the tinned goods of our modern civilisation lay the emphasis upon the quota of vitamins. This, esoterically speaking, is due to the shift of human consciousness on to etheric levels. Paralleling the growth of modern knowledge as to the "soul as intellect", we find a growth of understanding as to "the soul as life", though it remains as yet the great and apparently insoluble mystery.

There are two happenings of close and imminent occurrence. Today the bulk of human beings are polarised on the lower levels of the astral plane, but are conscious in the physical body. This distinction must be studied. Soon, many will be conscious in the vital body and beginning to be conscious on the higher levels of the astral plane, and some few upon the mental plane. But large numbers of people today are ready to be fully conscious in the astral body and polarised either on the mental plane entirely or centred in the soul. This produces the wonder and the difficulty of the present time.

Through the scientific ritual of meditation (for that is what it really is) this refocussing can be brought more rapidly about. Through the scientific culture of the ritual of service it can be still further developed. The ritual of the solar system is the result of the meditation of God and the act of divine service, carried on throughout the entire period of manifestation. The subordination of the lower life to the ritual of service is literally the tuning-in of the individual to the rhythm of the life, heart and mind of God Himself. From that tuning-in, automatically a spiritual development follows.

EPI 363-75

* * * * * * * *

...with the entering in of a new ray, and the commencement of a new era comes ever a period of much disruption until the forms that be have adapted themselves to the new vibration. In that adaptation those who have cultivated pliability and adaptability, or who have that for the personality ray, progress with less disruption than those more crystallized and fixed.

Particularly now should pliability and responsiveness of form be aimed at, for when He Whom we all adore comes, think you His vibration will not cause disruption if crystallization is present? It was so before; it will be so again.

Cultivate responsiveness to the Great Ones, aim at mental expansion and keep learning. Think whenever possible in terms abstract or numerical, and by loving all, work at the plasticity of the astral body. In love of all that breathes comes capacity to vibrate universally, and in that astral pliability will come responsiveness to the vibration of the Great Lord.

WM 265

* * * * * * * *

Training for new age discipleship is provided by the *Arcane School*. The principles of the Ageless Wisdom are presented through esoteric meditation, study and service as a *way of life*.

Write to the publishers for information.